Read October 2015.

Island Life
A History of Looe Island

David Clensy

In Memory of Babs

© 2006 by David Clensy. All rights reserved.

ISBN 978-1-4116-8917-6

www.looeisland.com

Chapter 1
The End:
Such an English Goodbye

IT was a bright and warm morning, the last day of August for 2003, and mist was flowing down the Looe valley and over into the sea.

I stepped off West Looe quay and into the sturdy little boat, the Lisa K., to be met by the weather-worn, familiar face of ferryman Dave Gardener.

Things were changing, he told me. He rarely takes people to the island these days – he concentrates on giving tourists short boat trips around it.

"They don't have time to be dealing with tourists," he said. "Not with Babs as ill as she is."

He fixed me with a sombre stare – as if to warn me of the days to come.

"Nothing of her now," he said. "Didn't expect her to see September, if I'm honest, but she's a strong one."

He turned the key and the engine chugged into life, and spluttering, pushed us out of the river, and into the misty sea.

For a time the sound of the engine filled the scene. Everything around the immediate calm water was obscured, with only the occasional break in the mist revealing the outlines of a wider world – the eerie shape of a cormorant standing on a rock, its wings outstretched to dry; the bobbing glimmer of a lonely buoy taunting us from the distance.

Then the mist receded like a theatre curtain, and the scene was set, as the island appeared before us.

Its familiar green arc of trees; its steady sandy toes dipping into the motionless water – memories of so many summers danced through my mind at the sight of it. But now the island stood quiet; shrouded and sombre.

There was nobody to meet us at the jetty – only Nelson and Lucy, the two ageing Collie-cross dogs, whose tails wagged so far their entire rear-ends moved.

Everywhere was eerily quiet. The Lisa K. chugged back out, away from the jetty, and disappeared into the mist.

I had visited the island each year since being taken there as a toddler by my parents, and I knew every nook and cranny; every tree and rock.

Roselyn Atkins – known affectionately as Babs – and her elder sister Evelyn – known to all as Attie – bought St George's Island, or Looe Island as it's more commonly known, in 1964 for just £20,000.

Two single ladies, approaching middle-age even then, they took on the challenge of island life with inspirational vigour.

The pair moved from their native Surrey, and Babs was appointed headmistress at a school in Looe. They faced the island's hardships, and were rewarded with a peaceful retreat from the outside world, and with the daily challenges of living so close to nature's raw fury.

For almost all of the next four decades the siblings lived alone on the island, more than a mile from the mainland, on just 22.5 acres of natural splendour – seashore, wind-beaten grassland, and densely wooded hill.

Attie recorded their adventures in two books: We Bought An Island, and Tales From Our Cornish Island.

Even as a young schoolboy I would sit engrossed in the stories – charmed by island life, and by the steely resolve and delicate humour of the two ladies.

As soon as I was old enough to wander away from home alone, I wrote to Attie and Babs, and asked if I could visit them, and help them with their island chores.

Ever since, the flush of summer meant just one thing to me – the chance to catch the train down to Cornwall, and stay on the island.

It was a chance to get back to nature. To live in a more inspiring world – windswept and interesting.

It was a place without mains electricity or running water, where the chug of the diesel generator marked the hours when you could use an electric light, where a tapped natural spring offered the only drinking water, and where flushing a toilet meant taking a bucket of seawater in with you.

It seemed a long way from my native suburban Merseyside. It seemed a long way from anywhere. But by the summer of 2003 it felt like a second home.

I carried my bags up to the old hut, which had housed me for so many summers, and started to wander around.

I eventually found Sheila at the back of the visitors' centre. Fellow island enthusiasts, Sheila and Gus Ravine had moved into the island's oldest building, Smuggler's Cottage, just a few years before, to help Babs with the day-to-day running of the island, after the death of Attie in 1997.

Now it seemed time was running out for Babs too. Leukaemia was attacking my old friend, and I could tell from Sheila's fretful knotted brow that the end was drawing near.

We all knew it would not only be the end for Babs – but for the whole way of life that the sisters had eked-out off the Cornish coast.

The future of the island's natural wonders seemed secure – Babs had already signed the island over to the Cornwall Wildlife Trust to ensure it would never become an off-shore casino or a movie star's helipad.

The island was now clearly worth millions of pounds, and the summer after Attie's death had seen a steady flurry of day visitors with beady eyes, and whispered messages of interest from ageing rock stars and over-paid racing drivers.

But the money was an academic matter to Babs. After a sudden loss of faith in the National Trust (when they went through a phase of selling off properties to the highest bidder in the late 1990s), Babs had signed it over to the Cornwall Wildlife Trust, with the ardent promise that she would "haunt the lot of them" if they changed her island for the worse.

Now she lay dying in Jetty Cottage – the room behind the ramshackle visitors' centre, where Attie had once retreated to write her books.

Sheila took me round to see her. Babs was on a make-shift bed beneath the window – a 1960s bed-settee, which did not need to be converted to accommodate Babs' now tiny frail figure.

She looked so thin and delicate, it seemed her body disappeared beneath the blankets, hardly leaving a visible shape.

Her eyesight was failing, and she looked up at me through misty cataracts with a faint smile.

"She has to leave the island and go to Deriford every couple of weeks for a blood transfusion," Sheila whispered. "She's not sure she'll have the strength to go again next week."

But with a valiant effort, Babs remained chirpy and sociable while I stood beside her. She would only admit to suffering from shingles.

"I fell over three weeks ago and bruised my eye and my arm," she said, apologising for the way she looked.

I talked to her briefly, told her I was working for another newspaper, but her strength was clearly fading, so we left her to sleep.

The week passed slowly without any day visitors coming to the island, and my brother and I did what manual work we could to help Sheila and Gus, who looked so worn-out themselves.

I tried to fish, but caught nothing, and spent long periods just staring at the waves, and watching the bobbing head of a seal in the bay.

Sheila whispered about the days and weeks ahead, and told me they planned to bury Babs on the island when the time came. It had always distressed Babs that the undertakers had dismissed burying Attie on the island as "impossible" – she now rested on the hillside above West Looe.

Sheila and Gus had broached the subject with Babs, and put her mind at rest on the matter.

"Do you think Attie will mind?" Babs had asked Gus one night. He told her she wouldn't, adding: "You can keep in touch on the ship-to-shore."

Our last week with Babs came to an abrupt end after just five days. I received a call on my mobile phone from Dave Gardener, warning of a vicious easterly gale on its way in.

"If you don't get off today, I can't say how long you'll be stuck out there," he added.

It had become something of an island tradition for the weather to rush us off at the end of our stay.

We had just one hour to pack, and say our goodbyes. Only this time we knew the goodbyes would be much more profound. In a way the rush made it so much easier.

Sheila left my brother and I in the room alone with Babs. I explained the situation with the easterly gale, as she looked up at me with blind eyes.

She squeezed my hand firmly, although her own hand now looked almost skeletal, with just skin stretched across the bones.

Choosing my words carefully, I said: "I hope you're feeling better soon Babs."

It seemed like the only thing ambiguous enough to suit the situation, for I knew that "get well soon" would have brought an ironic smile to her lips.

I suddenly felt for the first time, that she was afraid to die. Still holding my hand firmly, she looked up at me, and said, with devastating finality: "Thank you for all your help, with everything."

There was a silence, before she added: "You will keep coming back?"

"Of course," I said, working hard to keep my voice firm. It was such an English goodbye.

We walked out of Jetty Cottage. I took a deep breath, shouldered my rucksack, and made my way down to the beach.

Sheila and Gus saw us off, as we headed for the boat. Sheila was sobbing.

"You will come back though?" she said, echoing Babs' words.

"Of course," I said again.

I gave Sheila a hug as the boat touched the beach behind me. "Good luck with it," I said, meaning the traumatic weeks they were facing. I patted Gus on the back, and climbed into the boat.

Gus put his arm around Sheila, who was still crying, as we pulled away from the shore.

I looked back, and watched as the island grew smaller behind me. I knew I was watching a world disappear, forever.

***

I returned to the island the following September. Babs was gone, and her grave was marked by a mound of gladioli at the top of the old daffodil field. Just out of the shade of the island's woodland, it is the perfect place to look down at the blue water in Jetty Bay.

Babs had died in April. Fearful of the impenetrable frosts, the people from the Cornwall Wildlife Trust had dug the grave before the winter, and it had waited empty for six months.

Sheila told me of Babs' final days. Though weak, she could still hold a conversation until a couple of days before the end, when sleep overcame her completely, and she slipped away in the middle of the night.

She died on a Tuesday, and the weather was so bad it took until the Friday to get her coffin brought out to her from the mainland.

Just 12 people came to her funeral. There was the vicar, the vicar's wife, a few of Babs' friends from Looe, and six burly Lifeboatmen, who bore Babs' coffin from Jetty Cottage up to the daffodil field.

The rain fell heavily and the sea was rough as they lowered her coffin. When they had laid her in the ground the Lifeboatmen released a slow-burning red flare, to let the people of Looe know she was buried.

For a few days poor old Nelson, Babs' most faithful canine companion, would not leave her deathbed in Jetty Cottage.

***

While Attie had been the author in the family, Babs had always had more of an interest in the island's past. It rather frustrated her that nobody had ever bothered to write a complete history of the place.

Each year she would promise that one day she would try to write an island history book.

A few years before she died she gave me a photocopy of her notes, as if she knew even then that she would never get around to compiling the history herself.

With Babs gone, I determined to knuckle down to the task. I dug out the photocopied pages she had handed me two or three summers before. The notes were fairly spartan – just a few pages with random dates and musings recorded on them.

I rediscovered the tapes of interviews I had done with Babs a few years before, and began the long and laborious task of trailing

Cornwall for references to the island in old books, magazines, newspapers, court reports, and other official documents.

Slowly a fascinating history began to come to life before me. It was a history that featured treacherous and swashbuckling tales of smuggling, of great sea battles unfolding around the island, and of centuries of devout monastic austerity.

Although it's never been fully recorded before, it seems the island has a wonderfully rich history – with enchanting tales, fascinating folklore, and mysterious moments littered throughout its story.

In this book I will try to tell that story – the life of the island, and of the ever changing experience of island life.

Chapter 2
An Island Retreat:
The Monastic Years

LITTLE remains now of the island's days as a monastic site. For hundreds of years it was a place of spiritual devotion. But the only indications of this time are a few pieces of stone carrying distinctive masons' marks, which creep above the soil at the chapel site on the top of the island.

For all the time I spent there deep in thought, the wiry stubborn tufts of grass waving around me, and the sea stretching up towards the sky at the distant horizon, I simply couldn't picture the holy building that had once stood on the site.

Who were these men that lived on the island so long ago; felt the same breeze tussling at their hair; saw the same waves diminish in size for miles from the island's cliffs?

The seascape can give a simple connection to a little of their lived experience, but this slightest bridge of understanding merely fuelled my craving to know more about their world on the medieval island.

If I was to understand what life might have been like here before the Reformation, I would have to undertake a journey of my own.

So in the spring of 2000, I climbed aboard a train, heading westwards along the coast of South Wales. My destination was the monastic community on Caldey Island, off Pembrokeshire.

Caldey is a Cistercian abbey – a reformed version of the sort of Benedictine community that existed at Lammana – the monks' chapel on Looe Island.

The abbot at Caldey, Fr Daniel van Santvoort, had invited me to stay for a few days to experience a little of the lifestyle of a monk – a lifestyle that has hardly changed in the last thousand years.

But I was not the only newcomer taking the ferry from Tenby that morning.

***

"The problem is that there are hardly any Catholics in Wales," the abbot explained as he pondered upon a fact that had been worrying him for some time.

For Caldey Island, with its famous monastic abbey holds a contradictory place in Welsh society. It is often held up as a pinnacle of Welsh culture and history. Yet for almost thirty years its small Cistercian community had been completely devoid of any Welsh presence.

As dawn broke on the first St. David's Day of the new millennium however, things were about to change.

For the monks that line the choir stalls the day is already many hours old. They have risen in the dark of the night for their 3.30am Office of Vigils, spent a number of hours reading, praying and contemplating silently.

Now as they reach the end of their second Office, Lauds, the chanted psalms trip off their tongues with the dextrous comfort that comes from lifetimes of repetition.

Watching them from a pew at the back of the church is like looking at a painting; a moment of high realism depicting the romance of medieval life, and I could easily imagine myself transported back to a long gone chapel on St George's Island.

The pews stand in angular opposition to the choir stalls of the monks, and act as a place for lay-people (both men and women) to come and witness the Offices.

For the handful of women that live on the island this is the nearest they can come to entering the abbey, and a piously shawled figure is often silently present.

This morning though, the pews are empty, except for the bench in front of me, which is occupied by a tall, gaunt man in his mid-sixties.

As he stands, his heavy overcoat protecting him from the early morning chill, he follows every action, gesture and response of the monks. There is nothing in his expression of concentration however that gives away the fact that his life will alter dramatically, almost irrecoverably, within the next few hours.

Yet he is perfectly aware of it, for today Michael is to join this small, isolated Cistercian community, with every intention of devoting the rest of his life to monastic austerity.

Over breakfast he is no longer the incarnation of devoted piety that stood ahead of me in the church. Rather he is a charming, sociable and highly knowledgeable gentleman.

Born in Carmarthen, his first language as a child was Welsh. However an education at Cambridge and a life of managerial work in London have left him both looking and sounding quintessentially English.

His allegiance though is still very much with the Principality. As he chirpily butters his toast he tells me, with great pride, "I'm a Welshman, through and through."

The significance of being the first Welsh candidate for the abbey in almost thirty years, and of joining the community on St. David's Day obviously does not go unnoticed by him.

It was while he was a student at Cambridge however that he first began to feel a calling towards monasticism.

"I decided to cycle to the nearest abbey, and experience it at first hand," he explained whilst pouring the tea. "Much to my surprise, I found that one of the novices there was a contemporary of mine from school."

Over the years that followed this friendship has been a source of great support for Michael in his attempt to realise his vocation.

"I wanted to join a monastic community even then, but my parents were dead against it, and I didn't want to upset them," he said.

The usual preoccupations of life swept him along for the next forty years. Although he continued to visit monasteries regularly, it was only now, in his mid-sixties, that the opportunity for him to realise his life-long desire seemed to seriously manifest.

He had spent the previous 14 years painstakingly translating the account left by an Italian Contessa of her famous love affair with Byron.

"She'd written it all in French. I had a degree in French, so I thought, why not?"

With that completed, and finally in the hands of the publishers, he decided that it was now or never.

"I was very lucky to be accepted at my age – it's almost unheard of," he admitted.

As there was already a Brother Michael in the community, he would need to take on a new name. He had chosen Teilo, after the Welsh saint.

I asked him if he was worried about taking such a big step. He responded with a puzzled expression, as if the thought hadn't even crossed his mind.

"Of course not," he chuckled. "I've wanted to do it all of my life."

The island is an alluring place. It has housed monastic communities of many forms and denominations since the sixth century. The current Cistercian community on Caldey however was founded in 1929 from the Belgian Abbey of Notre Dame de Scourmont at Chimay.

I met the present abbot of the monastery, Fr. Daniel van Santvoort, in the simple cloisters that make the epicentre of the abbey. Originally from the Netherlands, he stands at well over six feet tall, and is particularly young for an abbot, in his early forties.

I was intrigued by Michael's future, and so over a coffee I asked Fr. Daniel how long it would take for him to become a fully-fledged monk.

He smiled briefly, as if the question had no simple answer, "Well, he'll probably be a postulant for about half a year, which literally means you postulate – you look around." He took a sip of coffee, glanced out of the window, and continued, "Then he receives the habit, and becomes a novice, for a two year period. The noviciate wear a white habit and white scapular, and each day have a class.

"It is a time for them to get used to the community spirit, and learn to work together. Then he will take his vows, over a three-year period - the vows of poverty, stability, obedience (to the abbot), and celibacy.

"Eventually then, after a five-year period he will take his Solemn Vows – that is, he will make the same vows again, but for life."

I couldn't help but wonder what could possibly make a person want to devote himself to such an austere life.

Brother Dominic, a monk for 53 years, and originally from New York, was in the US Air Force during the war. My airforce-style flying-jacket brought back vivid memories for him.

"It was when I saw my friends laying there, burnt and ripped-up – and saw the expression of relief on the faces of those that received catholic communion before dying, that I suddenly felt the calling," he explained.

I approached Brother Gildas, the unswervingly hospitable Guest Master, and asked him if tragedy was often a reason for joining the monastic community.

"It's something that we have to watch very carefully for," he confided through his impressive Marxian beard. "We have to be sure that it's not just a negative response to something like that.

"Of course, it sometimes happens that an occurrence such as that provides the impetus for a real vocation. We all have our own stories."

Back in the abbey though, the third office of the day, Terce, was approaching fast, and with it the moment when Michael would join the community. I met him outside his room in the guest quarters, preparing to leave.

I wished him good luck, and watched as he walked into his room. He picked up the sum of his worldly possessions – a small suitcase, and an overcoat folded across his arm.

As he stepped back towards the door, the sun emerged from behind a cloud, filling the room with tangible beams of light, and illuminating a few hanging flecks of dust that rushed sideways to avoid his path.

Michael paused, a resplendent silhouette against this golden wash. He took a sharp intake of breath. It was the only sign of nerves at this enormously significant, yet highly understated moment.

He then stepped out of the room, and casually walked towards his new life.

I sat for a time alone in my room as his footsteps diminished to silence. I had been the only witness to this life-changing moment; this tentative step across the threshold between now and forever.

The old, deep rooted oak tree that stood outside my window rustled peacefully, protected from the wind by the great white-washed walls of the abbey.

There was a distant sound of monastic chanting. The intricate harmonies of the choir stalls seemed all the richer for the addition of a Welsh voice.

***

It was a few months before I was able to get back to Looe Island. But when I did return I made the climb to the top of the hill, sat alone at the chapel site, and tried to imagine a monastic community, like the one I had met at Caldey Island.

I thought of how they would go about their daily life here, through their regular offices – vigils (or matins), lauds, terce, vespers, compline (or evensong). And how at the end of the day the sun would set over the chapel, as they chanted their latin psalms.

Later, as the sun did creep down behind the island's mound of tree-tops, I caught up with Babs in the 18th century barn – now known as the "craft centre", to quiz her about the island's monastic past.

She explained that the first Christian settlers are marked out as the earliest islanders we can now see when we look back through the mists of time.

"We think that the Celts were here, but we have no proof of it at all," she said.

A standing stone on the western slopes of the island, which appears Celtic to the untrained eye, has never been formally dated, and may or may not be as ancient as it seems.

"But later there definitely was a chapel, at the top of the island," Babs continued. "We know that was there in 1200, because we have the list of the chaplains to the island from 1200 onwards, which is on the wall of the Talland Church, just along the coast from here."

The list of "Chaplains of Lamana on Looe Island", as inscribed on a slate in the Sanctuary Window of Talland Church in the 1940s, offers a fascinating insight into the island's monastic life – the actual names of the chaplains who worshipped here from 1200, right through to the Reformation.

The inscription reads:

1200 Prior Helyas
1283 Andrew -----

1329 William de Trewidel – priest
1343 Adam Bryan – deacon
1348 John Doygnell – priest
1352 Richard Abeham – priest
1381 John Stangelonde – cantor
1388 Nicholas Walronde
1405 John Lyne
1433 Robert Symon
1456 John Wylt – priest
1457 John Tauton
　　-------George
1503 Walter Kyndon M.A.
1513 John Cocke
　　-------John Cole – cantor
1528 David Hengsley
1537 Robert Swymmer

This list was compiled for the inscription in 1942 by the Vicar of Talland, the Rev Timberlake. Some of the names were clearly lost to history.

But the monsatic presence at Looe was not confined to the island.

"From what we know, there was also a monastic chapel built on Hannafore," Babs explained. "But research has shown that our chapel on the island predated that, because two monks coming over to the island, to conduct a service were drowned, and the chapel was then under the abbey in Glastonbury.

"They then set up the chapel on the mainland, St Michael's Lammana, in the 12th century so visiting monks didn't have to face the bad seas – they would have somewhere to go in rough weather."

The monks also benefited from the new chapel on the mainland as it ensured they were able to collect gifts and offerings made by pilgrims, even if the seas were too rough to cross to the island.

The small dependent priory on Hannafore was owned by Glastonbury Abbey until 1289, after which it belonged to the Lords of the Manor of West Looe and served the neighbourhood as a chapel. It may also have housed a light for guiding ships.

The remains of the mainland chapel were excavated by C.K. Croft Andrew in 1935 when plans for a housing development threatened the site. The houses were never built and you can still see the outline of the chapel remains today.

So, why would the monks make such an effort to get out to the island to build the original chapel? What was so special about this strip of land off the Cornish coast?

As with all good Cornish tales, the answer is based in legend.

It's impossible now to say where the story came from, or indeed whether it contains any shred of truth (although most legends do have some basis in reality). But at some point in the first millennium AD, as Christianity spread through the Roman-occupied continent, and Romano-settled British Isles, a story began to gain favour.

Across Europe folk told each other that Jesus Christ, as a young boy, had travelled outside of the Holy Land, under the guardianship of Joseph of Arimathea.

In south-west England oral history has passed down to posterity a belief that Joseph visited Cornwall in order to trade with the local Celtic tin miners.

And folk in south-east Cornwall have always believed that he set the child Christ down on the beaches of Looe Island, where the child could enjoy relative safety, while Joseph visited the mainland, and did his dealings with the intimidating Cornishmen.

It sounds like a fairly tall tale, and one that raises more questions than answers. So what do we actually know about Joseph?

The Bible tells us that Joseph of Arimathea was later a wealthy disciple of Jesus, who, according to the book of Matthew 27:57-60, asked Pontius Pilate for permission to take Jesus' dead body in order to prepare it for burial.

He also provided the tomb where the crucified Christ was laid until the Resurrection.

Joseph is mentioned a few times in parallel passages in Mark, Luke and John, but nothing further is heard about his later activities.

Apocryphal legend, however, supplies us with the rest of his story by claiming that Joseph accompanied the apostle Philip (later St Philip), together with Lazarus, Mary Magdalene and others on a preaching mission to Gaul – modern-day France.

It is said that Lazarus and Mary stayed in Marseilles, while the others travelled north.

At the English Channel, St. Philip sent Joseph, with twelve disciples, to establish Christianity in the most far-flung corner of the Roman Empire: the British Isles.

The year AD 63 is commonly given for this event, with AD 37 sometimes being put forward as an alternative.

So Joseph clearly could have played a large part in the creation of our nation. It seems something of a shame that St Patrick is so revered in Ireland, for bringing Christianity over from Wales, but Joseph of Arimathea goes largely unregarded by the English, in spite of his claim for bringing Christianity to the kingdom.

The idea of Joseph delivering Christianity to our island, after Christ's death, seems more believable than the traditional legend of him bringing the child Christ to these shores three decades earlier.

Could it be that posterity and the handed-down tales of British folk culture, a kind of generational game of Chinese Whispers, which never seems to have been a strong way of holding onto simple facts, might have somehow mangled together the idea of Joseph bringing Christianity to Britain, with him actually bringing Christ to these shores?

If so, it is certainly an idea that has taken root in the culture of the British Isles.

It's a theme that has resonated through the art of generations of Britons, but is most famously painted in the words of William Blake's politically-charged poem, which later became a hymn sung by schoolchildren across the land – Jerusalem.

"And did those feet, in ancient times, walk upon England's mountains green? And was the Holy Lamb of God, on England's pleasant pastures seen? And did the countenance divine, shine forth upon our clouded hills? And was Jerusalem builded here, among those dark satanic mills?"

The Rev H.A. Lewis investigated Looe Island's theological history, and published his beliefs in two small works of 1939, The Child Christ at Lammana, and Christ in Cornwall.

He found the tales of the visitation of the Boy Jesus were widespread across the region. He writes: "In Cornwall it is found at such widely separated places as Marazion and Ding Dong in Penwith, St Day and Falmouth in Carnmarth, St Just-in-Roseland, and Lammana (Looe Island) in Wivelshire."

And perhaps we shouldn't be too quick to dismiss the idea of Christ's feet walking upon England's mountains green. Maybe the "countenance divine" actually did shine upon Looe Island's gentle coves.

As a merchant Joseph could well have travelled as far as the British Isles in his younger days in search of wealth. The people of the Middle East were highly sophisticated even 2,000 years ago, and today it is easy to underestimate the geographical extent of their trading links.

Trading with Cornwall's tin miners seems as good a way as any for him to make money.

And clearly he did make money – as is substantiated by his later ability to provide Christ with what seems to have been a fairly expensive tomb.

It is believed by historians of the period that Joseph almost certainly did achieve his wealth through trading in metals.

And in the course of conducting his business, he probably would have become acquainted with Britain, at least the south-western parts of it. Cornwall was a chief mining district and well-known in the Roman empire for its tin, while Somerset was renowned for its high quality lead.

Some Bible experts believe that Joseph was the uncle of the Virgin Mary and therefore of Jesus, and that he may well have brought the young boy along on one of his business trips to the British Isles.

Perhaps it was a means of protecting the child from a danger at home – whether it be the swords of King Herod's men, or whatever pestilence or plague might have been causing concern at the time.

And if Joseph was already familiar with the Britons, it would only seem natural, that later on after Christ's death, Joseph would have been chosen for the first Christian mission to Britain.

The trade between the Middle East and Cornwall would have been an ancient one, even in Joseph's day.

"That such a trade existed is too well attested to need proof," wrote the Rev Cyril C Dobbs, in his 1936 work, "Did Our Lord Visit Britain as they say in Cornwall and Somerset?"

"Herodotus, as early as 445BC speaks of the British Isles as the Tin Islands or Cassiterides," he adds.

"Pytheas (352-323BC) mentions the tin trade, as does Polybius (circa 160AD). Diodorus Siculus gives a detailed description of the trade. He tells us that the tin was mined, beaten into squares, and carried to an island called Ictis, joined to the mainland at low tide, which is generally held to be Mount St Michael in Cornwall, although some have identified it with Falmouth.

"Thence it was shipped to Moraix, and transported across France on pack horses to Marseilles. From Marseilles it was again shipped to Phoenicia."

The belief in an ancient passage of goods between the Middle East and Cornwall, long before even Joseph's time, was strengthened by the Harlyn Bay Disoveries – the oldest graves ever to be discovered in the county, found close to Padstow.

Some think these first tin workers were buried exactly like the pre-historic Egyptians, in a crouching position on the left side with the knees almost touching the chin (R.A. Bullen, Harlyn Bay Discoveries).

In her book, Joseph of Arimathea, Isabel Hill Elder, writes: "They are believed to have been the Hyksos, those Semitic descendants of Noah who left Egypt upon their completion of the Great Pyramid. Their knowledge of astronomy led to their creation of charts in earth and stone of the Zodiac.

"In no other way can we account for pre-historic Egyptian graves in Cornwall, and for a people with the scientific knowledge in pre-historic times to discover and instruct in the mining of tin, which later proved to be the most universally useful metal for the use of mankind.

"…It was certainly not by mere chance that Arimathean Joseph became acquainted with the Cornish tin and Somerset lead mining, for as a Prince of the House of David, Joseph was aware that his kinsmen of the tribe of Asher had made Cornwall famous for the prized metal."

She adds: "…Joseph should not be viewed as a lone figure on our shores in pursuit of his mining interests, but rather as a rich man of those days, travelling with a considerable retinue and with the entrée of the Royal Court.

"That the Boy Jesus was entrusted to his care by his niece Mary, the Virgin Mother, his eldest brother's daughter, is a tradition found in places widely apart, and tenaciously held in Cornwall.

"The legends concerning Our Lord's visits when grown to manhood centre around Glastonbury and the Mendip Hills, as persistent tradition asserts, and cannot be dismissed without blind incredulity.

"In folk memory these visits have been kept alive and passed on from one generation to another, held dear by the older inhabitants by whom it is not considered a subject for glib and sceptical discussion, nor for the prying of strangers out of mere curiosity."

As far as Joseph's journey to the West Country after Christ's crucifixion goes, it would seem somehow appropriate that he should come first to Glastonbury, that gravitational centre for legendary activity in the region.

Local legend has it that Joseph sailed around Land's End and headed for his old lead mining haunts.

Here his boat ran ashore in the Glastonbury Marshes and, together with his followers, he climbed a nearby hill to survey the surrounding land.

Having brought with him a staff grown from Christ's Holy Crown of Thorns, he thrust it into the ground and announced that he and his twelve companions were "Weary All".

Legend has it that the thorn staff immediately, and miraculously, took root. It can still be seen there to this day, on what is now called Wearyall (or Wyrral, or Wirral) Hill.

A cutting from the famous tree also grows within the grounds of Glastonbury Abbey.

The story goes that Joseph met with the local ruler, Arviragus, and soon secured himself twelve hides of land at Glastonbury on which to build the first monastery in Britain. And it was from there that he became the country's evangelist.

It is important to remember that Joseph was a Christianiser, rather than a civiliser. Ancient chroniclers paint a picture of the pre-Christian Britons, whom Joseph would have met, as self-reliant people, engaged in agricultural pursuits.

The Roman scribe Diodorus Siculus (who died in 14AD), described the native Britons as "civilised and courteous to strangers."

"They are of much sincerity and integrity," he wrote. "Far from the craft and knavery of men among us, contented with plain and homely fare, and strangers to the excess and luxury of rich men."

Much more was added to Joseph's legend during the Middle Ages. He was gradually inflated into a major saint and cult hero, as well as the supposed ancestor of many British monarchs, including King Arthur – another useful tool in determining a divine right for later would-be kings.

Joseph is also said to have brought a cup with him to Britain. This cup is said to have been used at the Last Supper and also used to catch the blood dripping from Christ as he hung on the cross.

A variation of this story is that Joseph brought with him two cruets, one containing the blood and the other, the sweat of Christ. Either, or indeed both of these items are known as The Holy Grail.

A much more controversial interpretation to the story that has emerged in recent years, reads Joseph's bringing of "the blood of Christ" to Britain, as bringing the blood-line of Christ with him – namely a son of Jesus and Mary Magdalene. But that's a whole other story.

What seems certain is that Joseph's later successors in Glastonbury's monastic community were convinced enough by the legitimacy of Looe Island's links to the Christ Child, that they went to these extraordinary lengths to construct and service a chapel on the island. Babs explained that the story is enshrined in the culture of the area.

"The legend of Joseph of Arimathea coming here with the child Christ, there's no clear authenticity about that," she said. "But strangely enough, the shield for West Looe, is a boat with two figures in it, one large and one small. And whether that has anything to do with the legend, we don't know.

"But there must have been a reason for a chapel to have been built on the island itself."

The tradition has continued to hold the attention of many ardent believers, even into the modern period.

Writing in The Cornish Times, of April 9, 1948, the Rev Paul Stacy, assistant priest at St John's, Glastonbury, gave a passionate account of his own belief in the story.

He wrote: "My father, Henry E. Stacy, was a Bristol artist who, in 1886, heard about Looe, then but little known.

"We went there for a holiday, and fell in love with it...We heard that on Looe Island was a reputed holy spot, but could get no answer to the question "why?" I have never even been on the island.

"I was vicar of St. Peter's, Coventry, for nearly 26 years, when in 1943 my health showed signs betokening that my work there was done, and that I must seek a parish where light work without heavy responsibility would be possible.

"Nothing, however, of the sort could be found, and meanwhile on a fixed date following my resignation with a moderate pension, but many books and some furniture, I should have to leave Coventry and go – nowhere! Being worried I went to consult Mrs. Tuckett (a relative in Looe); this was in January, 1944."

He continues: "It should be noted that, up to then, I only had a vague knowledge of the story of St Joseph of Arimathea, Our Lord, and the Blessed Virgin having come to Britain.

"Marazion (an obviously Jewish name) was known to me, and the story of the daub and wattle church and the Holy Thorn at Glastonbury, but I had no knowledge whatever of the actual facts, and had never read a word about it all.

"My surprise, therefore, may be guessed when a friend in Looe (but not a native) told me that the town was connected with the Joseph story.

"I did not believe him, but said: "You mean Marazion," but he insisted his statement. Then he told me that within the last few years references in books with some local traditions had led to excavations at Hannafore, where important links were unearthed, showing that Looe was one of the landing places of the Holy Family. This amazed me, as a complete surprise."

The Rev Stacy goes on to explain that the story haunted his imagination, especially on his regular visits to Hannafore Point.

He wrote: "I used to go daily to look at the scanty remains, think, and pray. One morning, when wind and rain were at their height, I offered a most unconventional and real prayer in the words: "O

God, make a man of me; blow away this nonsense; tell what to do and where to go; blow me anywhere."

"Then I heard an inward voice, but quite clearly and of insistent power – "Glastonbury, Glastonbury, Glastonbury."

"I said, laughing to myself, "How funny," and went straight back to write to the Vicar of Glastonbury making enquiries.

"His name was quite unknown to me, and I had no knowledge at all about him. He replied saying that he needed help, owing to a bad accident and would like to correspond.

"I came to St John's, Glastonbury, in June 1944. Then to my astonishment, I found that he, Rev Lionel Lewis, had written books on Glastonbury, and was in fact the chief authority in restoring and vindicating the wonderful tradition (of the Joseph of Arimathea legend)."

After a lifetime of writing sermons, the Rev Lewis may have had an uncanny ability for making a short story long, but he also clearly had a devotion to the Joseph tradition. And if he is capable of such pious devotion to the tale in the mid-twentieth century, it becomes a little easier to understand how devotees more than 1,000 years ago, could be swept along by the potential the tradition held.

He goes on to write of the strengthening of: "…my conviction that the tradition is solid fact, and that Blake knew this when, 150 years ago, he asked the question: "And did those feet in ancient times, Walk upon England's mountains green?"

"Consequently, much of my work here is to spread the story," he continues. "And help writers to make it known everywhere, for it is undoubtedly one of the ways by which we can inspire the Church, and indeed the whole of Britain and the English speaking people, with their Christian traditions and way of thought, life, and action to fulfil God's destiny for them.

"If England has, in a real sense, God's command to help to save Christian civilisation throughout the world, and to set the nations free in Christ, then the visit to this land of Our Lord, His Holy Mother, St Joseph of Arimathea, St Simon Zelotes and Aristobulus, and many other saints and national heroes who have enriched our history, will give just the inspiration that we so badly need today."

With passions running so high about the story within the ecclesiastical community at Glastonbury in the 1940s, it becomes increasingly easy to see how the fervour could have been strong enough to see a chapel built on the island, back in the medieval period.

So what do we actually know about the chapel? We know that it was built in 1139, and that a few pieces of ornately embellished masonry survive on the chapel site at the top of the island to this day. But it's difficult to paint a picture of a monk's life there from these pieces of 1,000-year-old rubble.

I asked Babs if there is any other way for us to try to understand how the island may have looked then.

"Well, there is a diagrammatic map of the island, and the coastline between Fowey and Looe, which is kept in the British Museum" Babs explained. "And according to this map, which came out in Tudor times, the island seemed to be dominated by the chapel. The chapel looked as large as the island."

Clearly the size of the chapel on the Tudor map could have just as easily been meant to depict the chapel's importance, rather than its actual nature. But it does give an intriguing insight into how the chapel may have been designed.

The map (Lyson's Magna Britannia) depicts the chapel as a sizeable church-like structure, with a sloping roof.

The building appears, like all churches, running from the west to the east, with the door facing east (traditionally facing Jerusalem). The chapel is also clearly depicted as having two small windows on the southward flank, facing out to sea.

The island itself appears to be barren and windswept on the map. The great crest of trees, which dominate the ridge of the island today, and are such a part of its modern identity, were in fact a Victorian addition. Like most islands around the British coast, Looe Island, would naturally have contained little more than sand, rocks, and grassland.

In the same way that the size of the building on the map could be seen as a depiction of its importance rather than its geometry, the style and substance of the design could easily have been born in the imagination of a Tudor cartographer. No one will ever know for sure.

What we can know more easily, is how a medieval Benedictine monk might have lived his life.

Clearly, he based his existence on the teachings of St Benedict. He spent his days in a combination of prayer, meditation, scholasticism and physical labour, set out by a regular routine, in much the same way as I discovered with the monks at Caldey – they are of the Cistercian Order, which is a reformed branch of Benedictine monasticism.

So who was St Benedict himself? Although not the founder of Christian monasticism, since he lived three centuries after its beginnings in Egypt, Palestine, and Asia Minor, he is nonetheless, one of the most important figures in European monastic history.

He became a monk as a young man and learned the tradition by associating with other monks and reading monastic literature.

He is believed to have lived from around 480 to around 547. His biographer, St Gregory the Great, pope from 590 to 604, does not record the dates of his birth and death, though he refers to the Rule written by Benedict as a guide for showing monks how to live. Scholars debate the dating of the Rule though they seem to agree that it was written in the second third of the sixth century.

According to St Gregory, Benedict was born in Nursia, a village high in the mountains northeast of Rome. His parents sent him to Rome for classical studies but he found the life of the eternal city too degenerate for his tastes.

So he fled to a place south-east of the city, called Subiaco, where he lived as a hermit for three years, tended by the monk Romanus.

Inspired by his lifestyle, a group of monks asked him to become their spiritual leader.

His regime soon became too much for the lukewarm monks so they plotted to poison him.

St Gregory tells the tale of Benedict's escape. When he blessed the pitcher of poisoned wine, it broke into pieces before him.

Benedict left the wayward monks and established twelve monasteries with twelve monks each in the area south of Rome.

Around the year 529, he moved to Monte Cassino, 80 miles south-east of Rome, where he destroyed the pagan temple dedicated to Apollo and built his main monastery.

St Gregory tells many tales of Benedict's life and miracles – which included mind reading, making water flow from rocks, making oil flow endlessly from a flask, and sending a disciple to walk on water.

After his death Benedict's brand of monasticism continued to flourish, in what was, according to Bossuet, the 17th century bishop, "an epitome of Christianity, a learned and mysterious abridgement of all the doctrines of the Gospel."

St. Augustine and his monks established the first English Benedictine monastery at Canterbury soon after their arrival on these shores in 597AD. Other foundations quickly followed.

It was said that St. Benedict seemed to have taken possession of the country as his own. Through the dedication of pious men like Wilfrid, Benedict Biscop, and Dunstan, the Benedictine Rule spread with extraordinary rapidity.

The life of the medieval monk would not have been an empty one. The arts, sciences, and crafts found a home in the Benedictine cloister from the earliest times.

The monks of St. Gall and Monte Cassino excelled in illumination and mosaic work, for example, and the Monte Cassino community are credited with having invented the art of painting on glass.

A contemporary account of the life of the Benedictine monk St. Dunstan says he was famous for his "writing, painting, moulding in wax, carving of wood and bone, and for work in gold, silver, iron, and brass."

Monks like Richard of Wallingford at St. Alban's and Peter Lightfoot at Glastonbury were even well-known fourteenth-century clockmakers - a clock by the latter, formerly in Wells cathedral, is still to be seen in the South Kensington Museum, in London.

The monasteries were clearly busy places – the engine houses of the feudal England of the Middle Ages – and for the Benedictine monks, holy places of peaceful retreat were maintained for quiet prayer and contemplation.

In the spirit of pilgrims, and with the ethos of "if something's easy, it's not worth doing", these retreats were often settled on difficult and remote sites – such as Looe Island.

Led by the teaching of Christ's own struggles with the deprivations of the wilderness for his own period of prayer and contemplation, the monks were drawn to retreats and sometimes, in extreme cases, individual hermitages.

So the medieval Looe Island may not have seen constant occupation by the monks. It seems more than likely that monks and perhaps even postulant and noviciate trainee monks could have taken on the trial of life on the island as an occasional spiritual challenge.

It seems equally possible that the island could have played host to at least one permanent resident who may have acted as chaplain to maintain the steady running of the site.

We know that by around 1200 two Benedictine monks, Prior Helia (or Elias) and Brother John, were living on the island, and that their job was to receive pilgrims, to maintain the church, and above all to pray and lead the contemplative life.

It has been suggested that they were also expected to keep a light burning in the chapel as a guide to shipping at a time when there were no official lighthouses.

The truth is, we just don't know the finer details of life on the island so long ago. But through piecing together strands of historical facts – the geography of the island, the architecture of the chapel, the few records of occupation that exist, and the psychology and belief-system of the monks, we can begin to build up a picture of how it might have been.

With the wind buffeting, and the waves lashing the spartan rocks of the island, and the whisper of quiet prayers echoing through the simple chapel on top of the hill, the island must have been a peaceful place.

But peace on the island wouldn't last forever. And its monasticism is only the start of the island's story.

Chapter 3
A Changing World:
The Reformation Years

THE island is impervious to storms. The sands may shift, and the trees may struggle, but the rocks and cliffs and grasslands will hold up to any tempest the weather can conspire against this wind-blown stretch of coastline.

But the islanders' way of life has always been more delicate. And there was a serious storm brewing in the early years of the 1500s.

Henry VIII's Reformation of the English Church, and the subsequent dissolution of the monasteries marked the final death knell for the island chapel.

But spirituality on the island had been on the decline ever since the Hannafore chapel had been built.

The island chapel had passed out of the hands of Glastonbury Abbey by the late thirteenth century, and by the early 16th century (c.1534) it had become a chantry, where prayers were said for the souls of a family named Courtenay, who then owned the island. This was a common practice among the wealthy who believed they could use chantry prayers to pass more easily through the gates of heaven. In effect, the church had been privatised.

The list of island chaplains ends in 1537 with the appointment of Robert Swymmer. By that time the chapel was probably rarely used for worship, although a local man accused of landing on the island for the purpose of piracy in the 1530s claimed that he was there on a pilgrimage.

Most early maps identify the island as St. Michael's Island; the Cornish had a tradition of naming island chapels after St Michael – especially where the chapel was on top of a hill (such as St. Michael's Mount in western Cornwall, and the chapel of St. Michael on Rame Head - which is visible from the island to the east).

But the suspected pirate's pilgrimage was to a chapel of St. George, who must have shared the dedication of the island chapel with St. Michael, and who would later be adopted in the island's name.

The monastic zeal was also waning nationally by the 14th century. Monastic recruitment declined steadily for decades – a situation made worse by the dwindling population during the years of the Black Death.

By this time many of the larger abbeys had become large scale landowners, and senior monks and abbots – who once were free to concentrate on maintaining the purity of monastic life – were now finding themselves being drawn more and more into the administration of the abbey's wealth. The result was a steady secularisation of the monks.

Abbots became obliged to serve the Crown – with 30 of the most important abbots sitting in the upper house of Parliament by the end of the 15th century.

The smaller monastic houses and nunneries maintained the simple life more effectively, and reformed versions of the Benedictines concentrated on the importance of a modest existence – especially the Carthusians, or Charterhouse monks, who stuck fervently to isolated and austere lives.

But the more general decline gave Henry VIII the perfect opportunity and excuse to initiate his own reforms of English monasticism – reforms almost certainly aimed at protecting his newly developed Church of England, as well as benefiting the Royal coffers, which were floundering after centuries of wars.

When the Dissolution was launched in 1536 with the Act for the Suppression of the Lesser Monasteries, it was presented as a positive reform of the monastic way of life.

The wording of the act even stressed the importance of the "great and honourable monasteries" where religion was "right well kept".

But it claimed other institutions were "sunk irredeemably in iniquity", and that they had "resisted all attempts at reform for 200 years or more".

The solution the act suggested was that the "…idle and dissolute monks and nuns who live in these dens of vice should be dispersed amongst the greater abbeys where they will, by discipline and example, be brought to mend their ways. The properties and endowments thus vacated can then be transferred to the king, to put to such better uses as he may think fit."

Under the act the property of any religious house with an income of less than £200 a year was transferred to the Crown.

At that stage compensation was paid to abbots, priors and prioresses, who were given pensions for life. Monks and nuns could choose to be transferred to surviving houses of their own order, or relinquish their vows and adopt a secular life.

Before the act, Henry's vicar-general, Sir Thomas Cromwell had been charged with making reports on every monastery and nunnery throughout the land, and he was rarely impressed by his findings.

"Manifest sin, vicious, carnal and abominable living is daily used and committed amongst the little and small abbeys," he claimed.

The act however was careful in its praise of the larger houses – whose abbots sat in Parliament, and whose assent would be required to pass the act.

Unsurprisingly, the act passed through Parliament without a hitch. Three out of every 10 houses were suppressed by the act, and hostility towards the Reformation grew, especially in the north.

In October of 1536 a rebellion, known as the Pilgrimage of Grace, was quickly crushed by the Crown.

Henry used the rebellion as a pretext for crushing those greater abbeys that had supported the rebels, abbots were executed, monks turned out, and the properties were forfeited.

The Cistercian abbey of Furness in Cumbria became the first of many institutions to voluntarily surrender to the King's possession in order to save lives.

In 1537 the Crown stepped up the Dissolution – monks under the age of 24 were banished, and the government encouraged brethren to make confessions against their superiors.

By the second half of 1538 nearly 20 monasteries a month were crushed, as Cromwell and his men toured the country bullying and cajoling monasteries into signing their own death warrants.

Those who refused were ruthlessly executed. The Abbot Whiting of Glastonbury Abbey, which had originally developed the island chapel, was one of the unfortunate ones.

He was dragged to the top of Glastonbury Tor on a hurdle, where he was executed and his body quartered – each quarter was then displayed in four local towns, while his head was placed on the gates of his own abbey.

The surrender of the abbey at Waltham in March 1540 marked the end of the Dissolution – there wasn't a single religious house left anywhere in England or Wales.

As a chantry, the spiritual life on the island may have survived a little longer. It was in 1547, under Edward VI, that a statute declared lands and revenues from "foundations endowed to benefit the souls of their founders (i.e. chantries) be appropriated by the Crown."

The statute, which made the Oxford and Cambridge colleges the only exceptions, would have been swiftly adhered to. The returns of commissioners from the Court of Augmentations recorded the purposes for which foundations were established. The court also sent out commissioners to compile inventories of all the goods belonging to the chantries – which included such things as plate, jewellery, and animals.

With the monastic way of life outlawed across the land, the island entered the quietest years in its history.

The weather continued to attack the cliffs, and the waves still crashed on the shore. But for decades the island played host only to the wildlife, the occasional fisherman taking refuge from the storms, or the odd pirate hiding himself away in the island's caves.

It's unlikely then that there would have been anybody about on the island to witness the most dramatic moment in the history of this stretch of coastline.

Every British school child has heard of the great battle against the Spanish Armada of 1588. It's one of the landmark moments in the nation's history, and the first strike of the battle happened just a few miles off Looe Island.

And the battle may have left a couple of mementos on the island as it passed.

During the 1999 interview Babs explained: "We have two canon balls we found here, which must have come from some battle. I always tell the children they came from the Armada, but whether they did or not is anybody's guess.

"The first battle was off here. We have a book on the Armada which contains a contemporary map of the time, and it shows the crescent of the Spanish boats, just west of the island, and the English ones staggering out from Plymouth, having played their game of bowls. And our island is shown, but it was called St Michael's island then."

And it was from the island's namesake and neighbouring St Michael's chapel, on Rame Head that the fearsome Armada was first spotted in the region, as Neil Hanson explains in his book The Confident Hope of a Miracle:

"For much of Elizabeth's reign, a hermit living in the ruins of the medieval St Michael's Chapel at the lonely outpost of Rame Head…had been paid to keep watch for enemy fleets.

"In these troubled times the watch had been augmented, no doubt to the hermit's impotent fury as his cherished solitude was violated, and two local men, John Gibbons and Henry Wood, were also paid 'for watching Rame Head…when the Spaniards were upon the coast'.

"A single beacon had been lit for the first of the Spanish fleet, but that and the presence of the local Justice of the Peace to confirm the sighting and order the firing of all three beacons to summon the armed militias to the coast were superfluous; Plymouth and the surrounding country had been alive with reports of the coming of the Armada since the previous afternoon."

It's hard to imagine now the fear with which news of the Armada must have been greeted by anyone standing on the island on the fateful day in 1588.

The execution of the Catholic Mary Queen of Scots the previous year had set much of Europe against England.

The Spanish army was the most fearsome in the world, and the armada that carried it towards our shores was so vast it stretched for miles. England on the other hand had a ramshackle pirate navy and a motley army with which to defend herself.

From the vantage point of the island, the threat of a Spanish invasion must have seemed very real as the great arc of ships emerged on the horizon.

The true dimensions of the threat were clear to the young Queen Elizabeth, as she demonstrated when she addressed the troops camped at Tilbury.

"…I come amongst you…being resolved in the midst and heat of battle to live or die amongst you all. To lay down for God and for my kingdom and for my people my honour and my blood even in the dust," she famously announced.

"I know I have the body of a weak and feeble woman, but I have the heart and stomach of a king, and a king of England too…"

The first shots were fired off Rame Head, within viewing distance of both Looe Island and Plymouth, at the end of July.

But these first strikes were indecisive, and on August 1 the Armada advanced along the coast in a sweeping crescent. The fighting continued all the way to Calais on August 6, where the Armada paused to wait for news of the Spanish army, which was due to cross the Channel from the Low Countries.

But the army had been delayed by Dutch rebels, and the English were gifted the opportunity to send fire ships into the tallying Armada, forcing them to weigh anchor and drift northwards, destroying the Spanish plan.

By the time it was heading into the North Sea the Armada was already breaking up, and the remaining ships made for their only hope of survival – a desperate attempt to escape by voyaging around the north of Scotland and Ireland, before heading back to Spain.

It was one of the most significant battles in Britain's history, and it erupted just a few miles off Looe Island.

But the island still had more than a century of peace and tranquillity to enjoy, before it would witness its next great tyranny – the years of the Cornish smugglers.

Chapter 4
Sinister Secrets:
The Smuggling Years

THE first year I stayed on the island as a volunteer helper, I was billeted in Smuggler's Cottage itself.

It wasn't the easiest place to live. The over-hanging trees of the woods left the tiny cottage damp and cold. The larger bedroom was consumed by the damp, and I would wake up soaked through with the moisture.

The smaller bedroom was out of the question, as the glass in the window had been smashed by a slow growing, but purposeful tree's branch. So the curtains were lifted up and down constantly by the free-flowing wind, as it circled the island.

In the end I chose to sleep in the living room, beside the roaring driftwood fire that I had made for myself in the ancient hearth.

Using the toilet involved a journey with a bucket to the landing beach to collect the flushing water, and I was kept company through the night by the constant scurrying of rats beneath the floorboards.

But I was more than happy to be staying there. Smuggler's Cottage had played host to some of the most intriguing moments in the island's history, and to sit beside the hearth in the evening, wishing the walls could speak, easily made up for all the hardships of island life.

The eighteenth century, when the cottage was newly built, and the early years of the nineteenth century saw one of the most romantic periods of Cornish history – the years of the smugglers.

It may seem like a swash-buckling, dashing era, with the benefit of hindsight, but of course it was all a bit of a cut-throat business at the time, and the region suffered from a great deal of lawlessness.

Contraband goods – chiefly alcohol with duty unpaid upon it – were smuggled into the area in late-night drops from ships in Cornwall's many hidden coves. The goods would then be stored in safe halfway houses – such as the famous Jamaica Inn on Bodmin Moor.

They were clearly unpopular in some parts of the country. Dr. Johnson defined a smuggler as: "A wretch who, in defiance of justice and the laws, imports or exports goods either contraband or without payment of the customs."

On the other hand the Scottish economist Adam Smith was more pragmatic about the practice. He preferred to think of the smuggler as "a person who, though no doubt highly blameable for violating the laws of his country, is frequently incapable of violating these of natural justice, and who would have been in every respect an excellent citizen had not the laws of his country made that a crime which nature never meant to be so."

Even in the twentieth century Daphne Du Maurier, who made Jamaica Inn universally known through her novel, defended smuggling – or "fair-trading" as the Cornish preferred to call it.

In her 1967 book Vanishing Cornwall, she wrote: "Smuggling is a word that too often suggests men with black patches over their eyes, clad in striped jerseys and stockinged caps, dragging kegs of brandy and rum into secret caves...the word is immediately associated with Cornwall, despite the fact that the practice was universal up and down the English coast."

She added: "Desire to thwart the law is a basic human instinct."

But the smugglers didn't always stop at this, and ship-wrecking sometimes became a more sinister ambition.

Wreckers would use false lights to lure ships onto the rocks – meaning certain death for the men aboard, but also meaning a fair haul of booty washing up on the shore for the wreckers.

Looe Island did not escape this era of romantic tyranny. While little evidence remains of wrecking taking place here, locals will still tell you that the string of rocks that sit just beneath the waves, beyond Little Island, were once used for this very purpose.

"That's what they say," explained Dave Gardener, who worked as ferryman to the island throughout the 1990s.

"Those rocks are called the Ranneys and they would be about right for wreckers. It's difficult to see them when the waves are squalling up. So it could well have been used for running ships aground."

Whether deliberate or not, the area around the island certainly had its fair share of shipwrecks.

On November 27, 1838, for example, the Bellissima ran aground on the rocks. Gale force winds were believed to be the guilty party on that occasion, and she was broken apart on the jagged edges of the island.

She had been en-route to Amsterdam from Odessa. All 13 men onboard were saved however, thanks to the recorded bravery of a boatswain Jennings, who threw himself into the turbulent sea to attach a rope to the stricken brig.

The island and the neighbouring bays have seen plenty of major shipwrecks: Wolf (1691), Ellis (1751), Speedwell (1786), Tregothick (1786), Unanimity (1802), Rose (1809), Harmonie (1824), Jane (1827), Hart (1828), Konigsberg (1834), Bellissima (1838), Dart (1842), Incentive (1863), Albion (1872), Rosehill (1917), Zarita (1926), Silent (1927) and the Naiad (1931).

In fact the rocks around the island are no less dangerous today, as Brixham Coastguard's records for December 18, 2000, display.

The Coastguard received a mayday alert at 6.07pm from the 28ft fishing vessel Arrant which became stranded on rocks on the west side of Looe Island along with the 31ft fishing vessel Marigold, which had gone to the assistance of Arrant and ended up "washed over rocks sitting in water, but likewise stranded."

Brixham Coastguard scrambled the rescue helicopter from the Royal Naval base at Culdrose, tasked the Looe Coastguard Rescue Team, and requested the launch of the Looe inshore lifeboat along with the Fowey lifeboat.

The Looe lifeboat arrived on the scene at 6.21pm and was able to get Arrant clear of the rocks. The records state that "the vessel retained steering and power and appeared to be sound."

Fowey lifeboat assisted the Marigold, and both vessels were escorted or towed to local boat yards for checks.

Brixham Coastguard Watch Manager Alf Tupper said: "Luckily for both these vessels the RNLI lifeboats were able to get to the scene within minutes of the mayday and so averted any injury or further damage."

And the Ranneys, on the eastern side of the island, continue to cause problems for boats – problems considered serious enough for a lightship to visit in the summer of 2004 to deposit a new light-buoy.

Another shipwreck on the island, probably more than two hundred years earlier, inspired the writer Wilkie Collins to pen The Rats of Looe Island, a short story in the 1851 collection Rambles Beyond the Railway.

He wrote: "About a mile out at sea, to the southward of the town, rises a green triangular shaped eminence, called Looe Island. Here, many years ago, a ship was wrecked. Not only were the sailors saved, but several free passengers of the rat species, who had got on board, nobody knew how, where, or when, were also preserved by their own strenuous exertions, and wisely took up permanent quarters for the future on the terra firma of Looe Island."

He went on: "In the process of time, and in obedience to the laws of nature, these rats increased and multiplied exceedingly; and being confined all round within certain limits by the sea, soon became a palpable and dangerous nuisance."

The solution hatched by the people of Looe, according to Wilkie, was to eat the offending rodents.

"All the available inhabitants of the town called to join in the great hunt," he wrote. "The rats were caught by every conceivable artifice; and, once taken, were instantly and ferociously smothered in onions; the corpses were then decently laid out on clean dishes, and straightway eaten with vindictive relish by the people of Looe."

The writer went on to insist that the tale was true. I can't help but hope it was. I stayed as a guest on the island for many weeks through the 1990s, and experienced the influx of rats that the island endured during that period – when bin bags couldn't be left outside over night, without the contents being ripped apart by tiny teeth.

I don't know why we never reverted to a culinary extermination ourselves.

But rats and wreckers aside, the tenants of the island in the eighteenth century were seen by the taxmen as smuggling vermin themselves.

After the reformation, the island passed to the Mayows in the 16th century. In 1729 Philip Mayow is recorded as having passed it to his son Burthogge Mayow.

The island was bought by Governor Edward Trelawny in 1743, together with Tolgover, near Looe, for a "trifling consideration". The new owner had been MP for West Looe in 1724 and 1727, was appointed a Commissioner of Customs in 1732 and was Governor of Jamaica from 1736 to 1752. The island remained in the Trelawny family for generations.

It was the Trelawny's tenants who ran the trade in smuggled goods from the Channel Islands to Looe for more than 80 years from the 18th into the 19th century.

The Hooper and Fynn (sometimes spelt Finn) families were smugglers who lived on the island from the 1790s to the mid-1840s.

They rented the property from the Trelawny family, although documents verifying this were lost when the Trelawny archives were destroyed in Plymouth during the bombing raids of the Second World War.

The chief smuggler was Amram Hooper. Records of his baptism and that of his sister, Jochabed, are found in the Talland parish registers for 1800, although their births are recorded in the family bible under the names, Philly and William. The bible was discovered by Barbara Birchwood-Harper, curator of Looe Museum, during recent research into the subject.

The baptismal names come from Exodus and a dry leaf marks the page where the reader, probably their father, Anthony, found them.

The Hoopers followed the Fynn family, who had been on the island since the 1780s, and there may have been a link between the two families, as there are entries of Fynn in the Hooper family bible.

At the time of writing (2004), a discussion group exists on the internet, led by the smuggling history enthusiast George Pritchard, which attempts to make sense of the smuggling history of the island.

George writes: "A family called Finn or Fynn lived on Looe Island for about 40 years from the 1780s. John Fynn's death is recorded in the Morval church registers. George Finn and Elizabeth also appear.

"Then, in 1789, a widow called Elizabeth Christopher, married Anthony Hooper and, in addition to the records of her three children by her previous marriage, we find her two children by Hooper, called Philly and William but later christened Amram and Jochabed at Talland church in 1800.

"They were the smuggling family of Hoopers. So, we have rumours of Fynn and Black Joan on the Island and then tales of Amram Hooper, he was in action from about the 1820s, he married in 1823 and was living in Looe in the 1841 census but his mother had remained on the island and died in 1841."

Both Jochabed and Amram were registered at Talland on June 25, 1800. But Jochabed is believed to have been born on April 28, 1790, while her brother was born on November 21, 1795.

The baptism entry for Amran and Jochabed is unique in its detail:

"Amram and Jachabed [sic], the son and daughter of Anthony Hooper of Looe Island, were Baptised at Talland on the twenty-fifth of June, one thousand eight hundred, the former aged four years on the twenty-first of November last, and the latter aged nine years on the twenty-eighth of April last. Godmothers: Mary Kendall, Amelia Kendall, Margaret Hext. Godfathers: Revd William Hosker, George Blewett, John Penrise Esq., William Beard. Signed C. Kendall, Vicar."

These records are now kept at the Cornwall County Records Office in Truro. But a copy of them, transcribed by the Rev'd Timerlake of Talland in the 1940s, was sent to the island for posterity at some point in the latter half of the twentieth century.

The Rev'd Timberlake also wrote: "The fullness of the entry is quite unique for the period, and the inclusion of the names of the Godparents of the latter all, with possible exception of William Beard, who could be "Marine of West Looe", are certainly Country "Gentry" – Kendalls of Polsu intermarried with the Hext of Lanlivery. Rev'd W Hosker (snr) was rector of Lanteglos-by-Fowey from 1805, his son or grandson was vicar of Talland from 1844-58.

"I have tried to trace, and only find that Amram married Philippa Medland in 1823. They had a son, Benjamin (b.1827), who married (1857), Fanny Shapcott Honey, both then of West Looe. Both Amram and Benjamin are detailed as "fishermen"."

In fact Amram and Philippa had a total of six children, including an elder Benjamin, born in 1823, who died at two years old and a daughter called Matilda, known to posterity as Black Till – a name that echoes a previous islander – Black Joan – Joan Fynn, who lived on the island according to records in 1804, together with John Fynn – both were known smugglers.

Spelling names throughout the island's history can be a trial the final e in Trelawny or Trelawney seems optional and even the name Jochabed is spelt variously in different sources. The baptismal records from Talland record her as Jachabed – spelt with an "a" rather than an "o".

It seems ironic, but Babs herself always went under her nickname – not short for Barbara (as countless visitors wrongly assumed) – Babs was the pet name given to her as a young girl growing up in Surrey, where she was the "baby" of the family – hence Babs. Her real name was Roselyn.

When I knew her she was in her 80s, and despite the fact that she was more than half a century my senior, even I called her Babs. Her sister, Attie, of course derived her nickname from her surname, Atkins. Her Christian name was Evelyn. But to return to the smugglers.

Babs was fascinated by the Fynns and Hoopers. She explained: "They [the Fynns] lived on an island off Plymouth [the Mewstone]. And when he [John Fynn] died the family didn't like to move to the mainland, so they moved house and came and lived on the island here.

"And they carried on with their own form of smuggling. And then they [the authorities] put the preventive men on the island. Whether our house was that house, that was built for them, we're not quite sure. But we think that the Smuggler's Cottage – in fact we realise that the Smuggler's Cottage is one of the oldest buildings, apart from the chapel, on the island, and is about contemporary with this building [the craft centre], which used to be a barn.

"They're dated around 1720, we've been told by somebody who judges the age of buildings, but we haven't any confirmation of that at all.

"The island belonged to the Trelawny family at the time, and the present holder of the title, Sir John Trelawny, a good friend of the island, visits fairly frequently," Babs added.

The popular story tells of John Fynn having been banished to the Mewstone in 1774 for seven years and unable to leave upon pain of death.

The story is elaborated upon by Rev Stebbing Shaw, in his 1788 work A Tour to the West of England, which appears in Early Tours in Devonshire and Cornwall, by R. Pearse-Chop.

Rev Shaw noted: "South east of Plymouth Sound, at a small distance from the shore, rises a high crag called the Mew-stone, to this island about fourteen years ago a man was transported for seven years, where he quietly remained in due time without setting foot on other land.

"Leaving his habitation to his daughter he went to Loo [sic] Island, about thirty miles further in Cornwall. She still remains there, a widow with three children, her husband being lately drowned."

The Fynn family is thought to have moved to Looe Island around 1781-3 and continued living there for at least 40 years (according to Thomas Bond in his 1823 book Topographical and Historical Sketches of East and West Looe).

However the birth certificates of Jochabed and Amram suggest the Hoopers had taken up residence on the island by 1790.

Barbara Birchwood-Harper, curator of Looe Museum, attempted to clear up some of this historical confusion.

"Many have tried to suggest that Elizabeth Hooper, formerly Christopher was a Finn and maybe the widowed daughter previously mentioned," she said, "but Elizabeth's maiden name was Venning not Finn and in 1781 she was not a widow with three children – she was a wife with one child and two more to be born to her and her husband Benjamin Christopher."

Whatever the connection between the two families, it seems that tragedy struck the Hooper family in 1815, with the disappearance of 30-year-old Benjamin, Elizabeth Hooper's son from her previous marriage – Amram and Jochabed's half-brother.

A newspaper report from the West Briton of January 5, 1816, offers a "One Guinea Reward" for anyone who can recover the body from the sea.

The appeal reads: "Whereas the body of Benjamin Christopher, who was drowned on the 16-12-1815, near Plymouth breakwater, has not yet been discovered, it is hoped that whoever may find the body will give immediate information to his mother, Mrs Elizabeth Hooper, of Looe Island, who will give the above reward, and take charge of the body.

"He was about 30 years old, 5ft-10ins high, well made – fair complexion – very light hair, had on a blue jacket and trousers – blue frock, light worsted stockings and yellow silk handkerchief.

"Benjamin Christopher, who lived with his mother on Looe Island, had left there for Plymouth in an open boat with lobsters."

Whether Benjamin really was carrying lobsters on that fateful day, is now anybody's guess. If he was though, it would seem a terrible irony, after living among the inherent dangers of a family of smugglers.

I asked Babs whether there were a lot of legends around the smuggling on the island.

"Yes," she replied, thinking about it for a moment. "On the far side of the island, there is a big indentation, which leads to a cave which is about 30 yards long. It's big enough for you, at high tide, to row a boat into. It does get silted up sometimes. It depends on what winter gales we have.

"But on the cliff above that there's a large stanchion. And it's our idea that the smugglers used to come into this little cove and use this stanchion to haul their goodies up out of sight of anybody in Looe."

I went on to ask her about the stories of tunnels dug for smuggling, leading from the island to the mainland.

"Well there's supposed to be one from here across to Hannafore. There is a place there called Buoy's Quay, and it would be a suitable place for anybody to land. The story is that the place is riddled with tunnels – but we haven't found any of them. One is supposed to go from there on to Wallace Quay [in Looe]. And one fantastic one, was another one from here to East Looe. But the most fantastic one of all is one from here to Fowey, but it happens to be nine miles away. So, utterly ridiculous."

But Babs was most fascinated by the character of Black Joan [Black Till].

She said: "She is one of those who lived in Smuggler's Cottage. And when the preventive men were put onto the island, we understand there were some smuggled goods in the cave on the far side. So they wanted to get rid of the preventive men.

"She pretended that her boat had gone adrift, and she came up calling that she was losing her boat. And there was one preventive man here, and he looked out and saw that it was drifting away, so he got into his dinghy and rode out after it.

"As soon as he had set foot in that, they all set to, to load the smuggled goods and hide them.

"And another thing in a very old book, a copy of the Cornish Magazine from 1890, somebody had interviewed one of the old smugglers from here. And he said that the smugglers used to bring their goods here. And the people who lived on the island, Black Joan [sic, actually Black Till] and Amram, they didn't actually do smuggling themselves. But they hid the stuff for them, and they used to lock them in the cottage and hide the goods so that not even the smugglers knew where they were hidden.

"And there's supposed to be some of that buried treasure left here. Before I came to live here permanently, my sister received a letter from a clergyman who lived in the Lake District, and he said he had been in the possession of a map that had been in his family for many years.

"His cousin had visited the island, and thought that we were the right people to have this map. And so he had sent it to us. It's a very old map, all the S's are F's. And every time you touch it, it breaks up. So we have it hidden very secretly, and it does show where the treasure is.

"We once did have a young fellow here, who spent his fortnight's holiday digging in what we thought was the place. But he didn't find anything."

But in 1997, shortly after the death of her sister, Babs received a letter from a lady called Margaret England, of Clevedon in Somerset.

Mrs England explained that she was in the process of tracing her family tree, and that her late mother (who died in 1992 at the age of 85), had told her that they had an ancestor "by the name of Van Ran Hooper Dann, who was a wrecker of ships around those parts, and lived in a cottage close to the water, which had a window seat that leads to an underground passage."

She continued: "When the Customs men were about, one of the ladies of the household would sit in the window seat to disguise the opening with her skirts. I think I was told that the underground passage leads down to the beach."

The Hoopers however, were not the stuff of legend. There is plenty of documentary evidence to support their existence.

In fact sepia photographs exist of Amram's grandson James Benjamin Hooper, a local builder, together with his wife, Eliza May (nee Blight). Indeed descendents are still alive and well in this corner of Cornwall.

Tales of Amram, Jochabed, and Amram's daughter, Matilda, appear in various stories about the smuggling events in and near Looe.

These tales were largely found and recorded by Commander Henry N. Shore at the turn of the 20th century when there were still men alive who had served with Amram. He published them in his 1929 book Smuggling Days and Smuggling Ways.

Those interviewed by Shore recalled that Amram, and he alone, knew the places where the goods were stored once landed on the island. Cargoes which could not be landed were sunk in Whitsand Bay and retrieved later using a system of weights known as creepers.

The Hoopers are also believed to have used caves for the storage of the contraband.

Commander Shore, who used the spelling Hamram for Amram, wrote the following in 1899: "I have succeeded in quarrying out from official and other virgin fields quite a mass of interesting material relating to Looe Island and the enterprising parties who frequented the spot in days gone by.

"The "cave dwellings" wherein the trusty Hamram and his daughter imprisoned the spirits entrusted to their care were subsequently discovered - one accidentally, the other by a process known in the profession as "pricking". The position of both has been pointed out to me by old men who were "in the know".

"The story of the Looe Island caves and their guardian angels would make quite an interesting chapter of history," he went on.

"Alas all who could speak of them from personal knowledge have, since imparting their experiences to the present writer, passed away to the "happy smuggling grounds"."

An edition of The New Penny Magazine from 1901 features an interview with "Wisdom Penaluna", a Cornishman who prided himself as the "last of the smugglers". The name was a pseudonym provided for him by the writer of the day, for whom the escapades were still clearly close enough for him to feel a pseudonym to be a necessary precaution.

It didn't, however stop him taking and publishing his photograph – a dark, but intriguing glimpse back into the world of the smugglers.

At the age of 96, when visited by the unnamed journalist, Penaluna was able to recall life when the "fair trade" was still in full swing.

"That there telegraph was the end o' we. It killed the honest trade," he said.

Penaluna had himself spent twelve months in prison at the age of 26 - in "the year King William was crowned" (1830), after being caught smuggling.

But surprisingly he didn't smuggle alcohol or gold or narcotics, he chose to smuggle tea.

"Them was brave times," said Penaluna. "…tea sold in England at eight shillings a pound, and we could buy in Guernsey or Jersey at sevenpence.

"That was tidy profits. The year of the breaking out of the revolution in France (1830) I was over at Cherbourg, and I and my mate we bought a score of tubs of Hollands – that is to say, twenty-one to the score – for seven pounds. We brought them back safe to England and sold them for three guineas a tub. Made by that transaction £26. That's what I call fair trading.

"We got baccy at Jersey for sevenpence a pound, same as tea, and sold it at half-a-crown. That weren't quite the profits as there was on tea, but it was easier to dispose of. And one-and-eleven on a pound ain't to be sneezed at."

But things didn't always go quite to plan.

"At times," Penaluna continued. "There was rough dealings. I mind in February, 1816, there was a bit of a scratch. The chaps had brought over a famous lot o' spirits and got all safe ashore.

"The Customs men heard of it somehow, and two riding officers came out and called to their aid two light horsemen, and tried to stop the goods as they were being carried from shore to the distributing place.

"But the farmers all round came to the aid of the smugglers, and there was some fighting. One officer was thrown from his horse and had an arm broken. Some of our men were severely wounded. Search was made for them after the affair, but they were not to be found: they'd been hid away, and were kept till their wounds were healed. I reckon there was a hundred and fifty men out that day – our fellows and the farmers and their men."

And Penaluna admitted that his own efforts were not always a success.

"I were cotched that year George IV died. The worst of it was, we had to do with informers. The Government, they had paid spies everywhere: they had spies in France, they had spies on our own Cornish coast – more shame to Cornishmen for doing the dirty work!"

But Penaluna saved his greatest passions for the Hoopers and Fynns.

"The first of them was a banished man to the Mewstone off Plymouth," he explained.

"Why he wor [sic] sent there I cannot tell; but if he were to be ketched ashore on the mainland, he'd ha' been hung. So he lived till he died on the Mewstone, and there the Hooper I knowed and will tell 'ee about he were reared.

"The Hooper I knowed, he left the Mewstone, and takin' kindly-like to an island, he took to living on Looe Island – that's about eight acres, and off the coast of Looe; it belongs to Sir William Trelawny – always did belong to the Trelawnys, ever sin' it wor created."

Clearly this wasn't true, but it offers an interesting insight into the dominance of the Trelawny's ownership by the nineteenth century.

"He gave ten shillin' an acre for the island; in all four pound," Penaluna continued. "I hear tell it lets now for forty or fifty.

"Hooper, he and his sister [sic] Black Till they called her, and a boy, they lived there. Black Till was the clever one. Sometimes her dressed as a man, and her'd work like a sailor; but she'd put on petticoats sometimes – Easter Day, like enough.

"There was once a black man on that island – his head has been found and is put in a glass case now. But there! – I'm ramblin' away.

"Hooper and the boy, they went over to Roscoff in a fourteen-feet boat and brought away a lading of tubs. 'Twere cruel rough weather, and they was balin' all night long to keep the open boat afloat.

"They couldn't make Looe Island, so they runned into the mouth of Fowey Harbour, and up the little creek to the mill. They was that terrible tired out that they crep' into the straw in the barn and fell dead asleep.

"I reckon that was in 1827. What do 'ee think now of the miller? He went off same night and betrayed 'em, and Hooper and the boy was took sleep-drunk as they lay in the straw, and all the tubs were seized. What do 'ee think now should be done wi' such a villain as that there miller? Hangin' would be too good for the likes of he!"

As it was Penaluna reckoned that the miller's fate was bad enough. "He went down and down," he explained, because folk in the area gave up dealing with him.

"Well, you sees, there be a Providence over all," Penaluna said. "And the face of Heaven turned agin him, and he wor lucky that he didn't get trun'led over the cliffs.

"I reckon he knowed it mightn't be over-safe for he to go along the edge o' the cliffs after that."

In 1890, the Cornish Magazine ran an article by Commander Henry N. Shore, entitled A Famous Smuggling Craft. It included an interview with an unnamed old smuggler who had worked on the Daniel and William – an infamous smuggling sloop.

"The spot we were bound for was Looe Island, a nice quiet place, where you could land your goods and stow 'em away in the caves without being interrupted, and get them run ashore to Looe afterwards, whenever the coast was clear of prewentivemen [sic].

"It was just about this time, though, that the coastguard got wind of the dodge, and set a couple of men to watch the island.

"We had Cawsand men waiting for us on shore, stowed away out of sight, so that the coastguard shouldn't get wind of the affair.

"You see, in those days there was only one cottage on the island, in which an old man, called Hamram, and his daughter 'Tilda lived. They had a cave somewhere, but no one ever found it; and they took jolly good care no one should see them put the tubs into it – they always sent the chaps inside the house while that was going on.

"They were staunch smugglers, both on 'em, and the goods would lie there safe enough till a chance offered to get 'em landed.

They'd get a small sum for every tub they took care of – I don't think they ever got tubs brought across themselves – and that's how they made a living.

"Well, we had to wait at Cherbourg some time before we got a proper slant of wind. At last we ran across with a regular gale from the south-east, and anchored under the lee of the island about midnight.

"Now, that was the best of this spot – no matter which way the wind was you could always get shelter, one side or t'other; and after the goods was landed, why, we didn't care.

"There was a ter'ble sea running, the craft was pitching bows under and presently the anchor began to drag and we nearly druv [sic] ashore, as the cable ran right out to the clinch. Oh, it was a dre'ful night, to be sure! I made sartin [sic] we should have to swim for it.

"After waiting for close on an hour, watching for the boat to come off, and seeing no signs of anyone, we launched our own, though she was little better than a dinghey, and set to work landing the tubs.

"My word, we had a job! But we got them all ashore, without losing a tub. There wasn't a soul on the island, barring Hamram and 'Tilda – our chaps had gone home, thinking we'd run into another spot to land. However, they soon got the tubs carried up with their donkey, and stowed away safe.

"As it happened, things couldn't have turned out better for us. For although our two chaps weren't there, we had the place all to ourselves. It was pay-day with the coastguards, and they'd all gone ashore to Looe, and it was blowing so hard they couldn't get off again that night.

"That was a good job for us! It was close on to four o'clock of the morning before we got everything clear; and dre'ful work it was, in a devil of a sea, and with nothing but a small boat to land in.

"As it was, she pretty nigh got her bow knocked out of her, and she leaked so bad we had to pass a line round her to keep the planks together the last trip we made.

"Directly everything was clear we slipped our cable and ran round to Plymouth – the wind had shifted, you see. But before we could get under weigh the boat had her bow pulled clean out of her, and she drifted ashore, somewhere by Downderry, I believe.

"Did I say we saved all the tubs? Well, then, I lied! For two were washed out of the boat while we were landing them, and were picked up afterwards by the coastguard on the beach near Looe.

"When we were abreast of Cawsand we were boarded by Mr. Foote, the officer stationed there, to search us for a double bottom – he'd information against us, you see.

"He found nothing, though, of course, he knew well enough what we'd been after. The fact was some one had informed against us, and if it hadn't been for the pay-day at Looe, and the boatmen not being able to get off to the island, we should have been nabbed, sure enough.

"Some of our friends had sent a boat across to Cherbourg with a letter telling us that information was out against us. We saw the boat pass, but took no notice of her, not knowing where it was bound to; and as the chaps aboard her didn't know our craft we heard nothing of the affair till we got back.

"The man who informed was a labourer by name of Sparkes, living at Millbay, who had a lot of private places about the country, and made a good bit of money by keeping tubs for parties. He wanted to get into the revenue cutter, and so he gave the information to the officer at Looe. However, he got nothing by it, for you see, we saved all our goods.

"The morning after we'd landed the cargo the coastguard came off to the island, almost before Hamram had properly cleared up his place after stowing away the tubs.

"You see, they had dead information against us, even if it hadn't been for their finding the boat and the two tubs we'd lost, and they searched and dug over the island for days, but they found nothing.

"The tubs – there were three hundred of 'em – lay in the caves on Looe Island for three months, before there was a chance of running them.

"Now, that was the only trip I ever made in the "Daniel and William", but there's no doubt she was one of the most notorious smuggling craft on the coast.

"Did I ever see the caves? No! Why, now, it would never have done to let people into the secret. It mightn't have mattered for once, but in the long run some blackguard would have been sure to have informed agin [sic] Hamram, and then the game would have been up.

"What's more, the caves never were found, the secret died along with 'em."

But the Hoopers' ingenuity for avoiding the revenue men while on the island, has become the stuff of legend.

Some historians believe that the brother and sister may have been helped by a signaller on the mainland called Fiddik, who would send messages with a lantern from Hannafore, from atop of his white horse.

With their signalmen, tunnels, caves and cunning, the Hoopers continually out-witted the revenue men.

The Government eventually decided to plant a preventive station on the island itself to stop the Hoopers' work.

The New Penny Magazine journalist in 1901 described the ensuing farce as "a cat watching a mouse".

But the Hoopers would not be beaten. The boy was now employed solely to watch the watcher – the preventive man.

All the business of smuggling continued on the island, only now it happened while the preventive officer was asleep.

On one occasion a smuggling vessel ran boldly to the island and discharged her cargo. The one preventive man could not approach, because a ring of men kept him at a distance.

However the proceeding had been observed from the shore, and a preventive boat was sent out, but did not reach the island until the vessel had spread sails and departed.

The New Penny Magazine painted a picture of the scene that followed:

"The premises of the Hoopers were searched – nothing was to be found. Black Till sat over the fire smoking; Hooper himself stood listless, with his hands in his pockets. The officers ransacked the barn, the outhouses, every portion of the dwelling – and found nothing. They could not swear that the ship had discharged run-goods, and nothing savouring of contraband was to be detected. Annoyed and angry, they departed.

"In fact, there were numerous subterranean passages, so carefully concealed that to the present day only one has been discovered, and that by the giving away of a portion of the floor of the barn."

Another possible tunnel exists close to the Jetty. Around the corner from the concrete jetty in the opposite direction to Jetty Beach, there is a small sandy cove, sheltered on both sides by upright and pointed rocks. The cliff face at the end of this small cove, has long been artfully covered with a wall of stones.

This wall existed before Babs and Attie moved to the island in the 1960s, and Babs once told me that a geo-physics student had ascertained that a tunnel or a cave runs back for a few yards beneath the island at that point.

The idea that the Hoopers' tunnels existed beneath the island barn – currently called the Craft Centre, or Jetty Cottage – is confirmed in A Book of Cornwall, by S. Baring-Gould, which was first published in 1899.

The author states: "A few years ago, when a picnic party went to the island and were allowed the barn to feed in, as a drizzle had come on, suddenly the floor collapsed, and it was thus discovered that beneath was a cellar for the accommodation of spirits that were not intended to pay duty."

This story was confirmed when the Atkins sisters received a visit from a Mr Pearn in 1965. He had been present at the picnic at the age of 10, and was able to show Babs and Attie the place in the Craft Centre where the tunnel had opened up.

But to return to the story of the thwarted preventive men and the cargo landed behind the ring of men. The job was still not complete. The goods had to be conveyed to the mainland.

This is when the incident occurred with the "lost boat", which Babs recalled when I interviewed her.

The New Penny Magazine painted its own picture of the event, and once again attempted to write Till's accent phonetically:

"One day Black Till ran in despair to the preventive man, with tears in her eyes and wringing her hands. "Oh, lor!" cried she, "What iver shall us do? There is our boat hev broke away, and be now carried out to say. Do'ee now help me, there's a dear man. If that 'ere boat be lost, I'll go and drowned myself."

"The obliging officer ran to the cliff and saw the black speck of the boat tossing on the waves, and being swept out to sea by the tide. He at once jumped into his own boat and rowed hard in pursuit of her, and after some time succeeded in recovering her.

"Whilst this was going on on one side of the island, a party of smugglers was clearing the hiding-place and carrying away the tubs of spirits as fast as they could on shore. The officer returned, bringing the rescued boat with him. Whether he ever found out how he had been befooled I could not learn."

But the authorities were not always fastidious about trying to outwit the Hoopers.

Life became easier for the Hoopers with the arrival of the coastguard service and the arrival, in Looe of an Irish coastguard called Thomas Fletcher.

Fletcher entered HM Coastguard service in 1833. He came to Looe in 1834 and married a local girl, Elizabeth Higgins.

Smuggling was rife in Looe at the time and it was not unknown for coastguards and revenue men to sympathise with a trade, which was so vital for the local economy.

Whether by sympathy, fear or simply because it was a lucrative trade, Fletcher appears to have joined Amram's organisation.

Smuggling in Looe differed from the well-documented business in Polperro, run by Zephaniah Job with the apparent approval of the Trelawnys.

The smugglers of Looe left no records, only tales passed by word of mouth of incidents involving individual smugglers.

A Looe author, Elizabeth Steed Shapcott, writing in the 1930s, adds to the information available from her interviews with her father and an unnamed seamstress who supplied details of some of the happenings on the island.

Thomas Fletcher absconded from the Coastguard service and reappeared in Looe, as a fisherman in 1837.

Rumours abound that he, and the Hoopers were caught and brought to account for their activities, however, no evidence has yet been discovered and many files were lost after a fire at Fowey coastguard headquarters.

Both men are known to have lived to old age and were buried with walking funerals.

Amram lies in St Martin's churchyard, near Looe, and Thomas and his wife in Schlerder Abbey.

In the 1901 article, the New Penny Magazine journalist recalled: "The story was told me that when old Hooper lay a-dying he was offered as much as sixty pounds if he would reveal the secret of the hiding places. He steadfastly refused. "I'll die as I've lived – an honest man," he said."

Chapter 5
More Innocent Times:
Natural wonders and the Farming Years

BY the time Queen Victoria took to the throne, the Cornish smuggling trade was passing into the pages of the history books.

As the island was left to enjoy more law-abiding times, a peace descended. The natural wonders, and even the limited farming opportunities, would be enough to attract islanders through the second half of the nineteenth century.

The wildlife, and particularly the seabirds that have nested on the island for centuries, are the most permanent residents that the island knows.

To stay on the island as a volunteer during the nesting season, is to take your life in your hands. Every moment of every day you're uncomfortably conscious of the frailty of your skull, as gulls loom overhead, their beaks permanently poised to dive-bomb you.

The wise, and considerate, island visitor stays well away from Little Island – where the gulls nest to bring their young into the world.

But despite this caution, on more than one occasion I have heard the ominous swooping of a bird's wings, and felt a fierce warning peck at my scalp – a reassuring, if somewhat forceful reminder, of who really rules the island roost.

I have even been lucky enough to experience the altogether more tranquil delights of the cormorant nesting season.

They prefer to settle on the island's steeper western cliffs to welcome forth the next generation of their kind to life on the Cornish coast.

To peer down silently at them from above, being ever careful to not disturb their windswept peace, as they busy themselves in their dozens, fussing about with bits of twigs and nesting feathers, is a natural spectacle that will never diminish in my mind.

Such scenes have fascinated visitors to the island for centuries. In the late 16th century, when the island was owned by Master Mayow of Bray, visitor Richard Carew wrote: "A great abundance of sundry sea-fowle [sic] breed upon the strond, where they lay, and hatch their eggs, without care of building any nests, at which time, repairing thither, you shall see your head shadowed with a cloud of old ones, through their diversified cries, witnessing their general dislike of your disturbance, and your feete [sic] pestered with a large number of young ones, some formerly, some newly, and some not yet disclosed, at which time (through the leave and kindness of Master May [sic], the owner) you may make and take your choyce.[sic]"

These days, of course, the birds are protected, and their nesting is carefully studied by the volunteers of the Cornwall Wildlife Trust.

The later decades of the eighteenth century was a time of great change on the island. It went from being the seedy haunt of smugglers, to a sedate piece of farming land, tilled by a series of tenant farmers, and owned by the ancient Trelawny clan, who still dominate the Cornish aristocracy today.

Even the nature of the island is believed to have changed significantly. As late as 1870, the Lakes Par History of Cornwall, records that the "island bears no trees."

So around the end of the nineteenth century the trees, which now dominate the ridge of the island, must have been deliberately planted as woodland.

A Victorian photograph taken from Hannafore around 1890, with elaborately dressed visitors looking out towards the island, shows that the woodland was by then looking well-matured.

So the planting must have taken place shortly after 1870, when the island was recorded as being treeless.

The picture is also interesting because it clearly shows the island's three buildings. Smuggler's Cottage, with a very clean-looking perimeter wall stands out the clearest. But with closer inspection you can also see the distinctive gable-end of the main island house, and the rectangular outline of Jetty Cottage (which was originally built as the island's barn, and is now known as the Craft Centre or Visitor Centre).

You can also clearly see that the bridge to Little Island is in place on the photograph, and if you look very carefully at the Landing Beach on the northern side of the island, there appears to be the rectangular roof of the boat house (which was later destroyed and swept away by a storm).

The island, having been bought by Governor Edward Trelawny in 1743, remained in the Trelawny family for generations and when Sir William Trelawny died in 1856 he left the island to his eldest son, Sir John Trelawny.

Sir John clearly showed an interest in island life, as in 1874, he wrote a letter in the Cornish Times about the intricacies of seaweed cutting.

The previous year, 1873, the foreshore of the island had been purchased by Sir John, from HRH The Prince of Wales – presumably the land had, until then come under the Duchy of Cornwall.

Concrete evidence about life on the island can be found in the census of 1841, which records that there were two houses inhabited with three males and three females living there.

The census for 1851 records that the two houses were inhabited with four males and three females.

While the 1861 census records that just one house was inhabited, by three males and five females.

According to research conducted by Barbara Birchwood-Harper, curator of Looe Museum, in 1876 the Trelawnys inspected the site for a new house to be built. The result was to be Island House – the distinctive gabled property now so associated with island life.

But the island's troubled past did not leave the new islanders in total peace.

According to a lecture given in 1928 to Looe Old Cornwall Society, by local historian Elizabeth Shapcott, around the year 1850, a farmer and his wife lived on the island, and the wife awoke one night to see the shape of a man walk across the room and disappear through the wall. The apparition, which was surrounded by a bluish light, was said to have been very tall, aristocratic-looking with grey hair and very beautiful hands with long fingers.

In a chilling twist, some years later, a skeleton was unearthed on the island – the body, possibly a shipwreck victim who had been discovered on the shore and buried, was a tall man with unusually long fingers.

According to Shappcott another ghost on the island was that of a black man who had been killed in a fight and was seen with blood always streaming from his face.

Another interesting twist in the island's tale comes in 1874, when a detachment of HM Coastguard were billeted in Smuggler's Cottage. As a result, documents from around the time refer to Smuggler's Cottage as the Coastguard's Cottage.

With the infamy and intrigue of the smuggling years consigned to the pages of the history books and the ballads of folklore, much of the detail of life on the island in the later part of the nineteenth century comes from the fastidious court reports and newspaper cuttings, which follow minor misdemeanours.

One such report appeared in the Cornish Times of August 11, 1877. It's hardly the finest piece of journalism you will ever read. Indeed had I produced a court report of comparative quality during my time as a junior newspaper reporter, I would fully have expected to have been promptly dismissed.

But if we forgive the reporter for his basic grasp of the language, apparent inability to tell a story in the right order, and his disregard for prejudicing the pending case – which even in 1877 would have presumably been classed as contempt of court under common law – we can at least pick up a few interesting facts about contemporary island life.

The report reads: "On Wednesday at the clerk's office, Liskeard, before Captain Hawker, the Magistrate, Philip Hender, who is supposed to be of weak intellect was charged with stealing a painter, mast, and sail, at Looe island on Monday evening last, the property of W.L.S. Trelwany, Esq.

"James Henry Nicholls said that he resided on Looe Island, and was in the employ of Mr Trelawny, who keeps two boats on the island, and these boats were in his charge.

"He saw the boats every morning and evening. He saw them on Monday morning, and in the evening was told by Soady that the prisoner had appropriated the articles produced.

"He went to the boat the prisoner had with him, and found the articles in his boat, and he took possession of them.

"Edward Soady said he was a fisherman residing at Looe. He was on Looe Island on Monday evening, and had a talk with the prisoner for about ten minutes, at about six o'clock in the evening.

"He then saw the prisoner go to the boat-house on the island, and take the articles now produced and place them in his boat. He asked the prisoner what he was going to do with them, and he said, "What odds to you?" Witness then went up the hill and met Nicholls, and mentioned what he had seen to him.

"PC Westlake said he apprehended the prisoner about eight o'clock on Monday evening. He merely said, on being charged, that this was the third time, and the third time was lucky. The devil must have seen him, or he should not have done it. The magistrates committed him to take his trial at the next Quarter sessions.

"The latter part of the career of the prisoner appears to have been as follows:- In May last he was convicted of stealing a can of silicate at East Looe, for which he had two months imprisonment. On the expiration of his term of immediately after his liberation, he went into Byers's eating-house and stole a clothes brush, for which offence he was sentenced to fourteen days.

"He only returned from Bodmin on Friday of last week, when on Monday he was again apprehended for the above offence."

But for all of these scraps of evidence gathered from across the nineteenth century, the most illuminating record of Victorian island life comes from the reports of Liskeard County Court in March 1894.

It's a tale of gun-toting potato merchants, fainting women, missing rabbits, and embarrassed policemen. There is no better – or indeed more amusing – way of recounting the whole sorry tale, than in the officious language of the original court transcript.

However you must be a little patient with the account of the incident – as in the great tradition of courtroom records, it seems to have been written backwards.

By the very nature of judicial drama – questioning, cross examining, and the calling of various witnesses – the tale suffers from some repetition. But it also spectacularly opens up the world of island life at the end of the nineteenth century, in all its pettiness and mundanity (if it bores you, then you have the author's permission to move on to the end of the chapter).

"At Liskeard County Court, before his Honour Judge Granger, Joseph Williams, naval pensioner, claimed from his former employer, Ezra Joseph Neale, £5 damages for unlawfully entering and searching a dwelling-house in his occupation, and £2 8s, balance of a month's wages for dismissal without proper notice. Mr A W Venning for plaintiff; Mr Borlase Childs for defendant.

"Mr Venning, in opening the case for the plaintiff, said in August of last year, Mr Neale, who was a potato merchant, of 24, Thomas Street, Bristol, advertised for a caretaker for Looe Island, of which he was the lessee.

"Plaintiff, who was then living in Plymouth, answered the advertisement, and was engaged at 16s a week, with a month's notice on either side previous to terminating the engagement.

"On January 22nd last, Mr Neale came down to the island from Bristol, sent Mrs Williams to his house to prepare for his reception, and told plaintiff to row into Looe for supplies.

"The coast thus being clear, he sent to the shore for PC Holloway, one of the Looe constables, and wanted him to search plaintiff's house, saying he suspected him of dishonesty. But the constable, having no search warrant, very properly objected, and the defendant and another man who was with him then entered and searched the cottage.

"Defendant then sent for Mrs Williams, and on arriving at her cottage, she found Mr Neale turning the place upside down in search of the articles he said had been stolen. He turned out a gun and some cartridges belonging to the defendant and confiscated them, and on Williams' return, all the parties assembled on the beach, where a regular melee took place.

"Rough words passed between plaintiff and Neale, threats were made use of, firearms were even presented, and Mrs Williams fainted.

"Defendant then gave plaintiff notice to leave at once, and the man was turned adrift with only a week's wages in his pocket in lieu of the month's notice to which he believed himself to be entitled.

"Since that time he had been living in Looe, unable to find another situation, and he now claimed redress from defendant for entering and ransacking his house and for dismissing him without proper notice."

The report then goes on to examine the case in finer detail.

"Joseph Williams, the plaintiff, stated that he answered defendant's advertisement in August last, and saw him on the island on September 13th, when defendant showed him what he called 'The Island Rule Book'. That book had since been stolen out of his house.

"He agreed to observe the rules written there, and to live as caretaker on the island for 16s a week, with house and garden.

"As to notice, defendant wanted it to be only a week, but witness said he could not get his crops out of the garden in that time and stood out for a month. Defendant agreed to this, remarking 'Let it stand at that then.'

"He entered on his duties on September 18th, and stayed until January 22nd last. About 7.30 on the morning of the 22nd, defendant came on the island from the mainland, knocked at witness's door, and told him to fetch the luggage from the boat, saying he had brought a gentleman friend from America with him. That 'gentleman friend' had now got witness's situation on the island.

"After he had fetched up the luggage, Neale sent him off to Looe for supplies, telling him he should not want his wife till half past ten or eleven. While rowing over to the shore, however, he saw his wife go over to Neale's house, and it was then only about nine o'clock.

"When he had got back to the island he saw Neale and his friend on the beach, and his wife was fainting in the arms of Toms, the boatman who brought Neale across.

"PC Holloway was also present. His wife called to him that Neale and the policeman had been ransacking their house in his absence. He asked Holloway what right he had to enter his house, and he was afraid he swore at him, being excited at his wife's condition.

"Holloway said 'It's not my fault. I've done nothing wrong. Neale called me here.'

"Witness then made a step towards Neale, who took up a double-barrelled gun, presented it at witness, and said, 'You take another step, and I'll shoot.'

"His friend, named Simmons, also presented a revolver at him, which had been taken out of the house. Witness could do nothing in the face of the firearms, and went up to his house, which he found topsy-turvy.

"A gun belonging to him, two revolvers, the rule-book, and two of his letters were missing. The revolvers belonged to Neale, but they were handed to witness to keep. Even the bed and bedding had been turned over, and the pantry had been searched to see what he had for dinner the day before.

"He came out again and met Neale, who said, 'You get off the island today, or I'll chuck your things over the cliff.'

"He left that day, and had since received 16s, one week's wages, from Mr Scantlebury, of Looe, defendant's agent. From that time he had been living at Looe out of employ.

"In answer to Mr Childs, witness, having examined the rule book, declared that it had been altered since it left his possession. One of the rules there now said: 'No ferrets or guns to be kept on the island.' When he first had the book the rule said: 'No ferrets to be kept or guns fired on the island.'

"When he made his agreement with defendant nothing was said about his wife being required to give her services at defendant's house.

"At the back of his cottage there was a room in which nets were stored. They were defendant's nets, but witness had stored them there for his own convenience, and not by defendant's orders.

"No room in his cottage was reserved by Mr Neale for the convenience of his visitors. The gun in his house was one obtained on approval from Bawden Bros, of Looe, and his wife had put it away in his bedroom.

"He obtained it to shoot birds with, because he could not always get to the mainland for food, and his wife and he spent one Sunday on the island with nothing to eat. Swore he had never shot a rabbit on the island.

"The two charges taken from his cottage were two China discharges from the navy. Admitted threatening defendant and the constable too, that if Neale was the means of killing his wife, he would be the means of Neale's death, and he would have carried out his threat too.

"Messrs. Bond and Pearce, of Plymouth, acted for him at first in the case, and wrote letters (produced) to defendant and PC

Holloway. Re-examined, the gun had been handed back to him, after being kept a month, and that had prevented him from returning it to Bawden Bros.

"When he obtained the gun he bought a shilling's worth of cartridges, which were those found in his house by defendant. He produced Messrs. Bawden's receipted bill for same.

"Diana Williams, wife of the previous witness, stated that on January 22nd, after her husband had gone to Looe with the boat, defendant sent her to his house to get breakfast. After a time PC Holloway came over to fetch her, and told her, "Mr Neale has lost a ferret, four rabbit-nets, and 100 cartridges; he thinks you and your husband know something about it, and he's going to turn you ashore today."

"She replied that she knew nothing about the missing articles. On reaching the cottage, she found Neale there. He asked for the revolvers. She told him he had no business there while her husband was away, and he was not acting like a gentleman.

"Neale said, "You have a gun here; where is it?" She replied, "We have none of our own." He said, "And you've got some cartridges." She answered, "None belonging to you," and in answer to questions by the constable, she also denied having the ferret or any nets.

"The defendant and PC Holloway went into the pantry and the first bedroom, and proceeded to search through all the rooms, looking under the beds and turning over everything. All that they found was a rabbit-net which her husband had picked up on the island, and which the defendant said was not his.

"She herself placed her husband's cartridges on the table. Neale said at once that they were some of his, but when she denied it, he said they were "just like his". When they had finished their search, the constable said, "Neale had made a fool of me over this, and I'll never come here any more."

"On the beach she called to her husband that Neale had been ransacking the cottage, and then she nearly fainted. – Cross examined: Neale was inside and not outside the cottage when she came up. She wrapped up the gun and put it under the bed for no other reason than that she felt inclined to do so. Holloway gave the gun to defendant, who took it away with him.

"William T. Toms, the boatman who rowed the defendant to the island on the morning of the 22nd deposed that about quarter of an hour after plaintiff left the island defendant got into his boat and instructed him to pull over to the mainland, where PC Holloway was waiting.

"They took the constable on board, and returned to the island together. Defendant told witness on the way that he suspected Williams of having stolen a ferret and nets, and that if he did not leave the island that day he should "chuck his things over the cliff."

"On landing, the defendant and the constable, with Simmons, went to plaintiff's cottage, witness remaining near the boathouse on the beach, and then PC Holloway fetched Mrs Williams and they all went into the cottage. When Mrs Williams came back they all came down on the beach, and there was a bit of a row. The men were using "brave strong language," but no blows were struck. Defendant had his gun with him. Mrs Williams nearly fainted, and witness held her up."

The court report then proceeds to tell the story all over again, but this time from the point of view of the defendant.

"Mr Childs, for the defence, submitted that there had been no unlawful entry or searching of plaintiff's cottage by defendant, inasmuch as plaintiff paid no rent, and there were no relations between the parties as between landlord and tenant. When defendant engaged Williams as caretaker, he gave him clearly to understand that a spare bedroom and the room in which the nets were stored were reserved for the accommodation of his visitors when his own house should be full.

"So that, in any case, defendant had the right to enter the cottage and go through the passage to get to those rooms. Defendant also had justification for making a search, because he had found shot rabbits on the island. He should prove, too, that neither defendant nor PC Holloway entered the cottage until they received express permission of plaintiff's agent, his wife.

"And no search took place and the cottage was not ransacked, because the wife herself produced the articles in question.

"As to the second claim for dismissal with insufficient notice he should produce witnesses who would show that Williams had many times referred to himself as being a "weekly" man, and the distinct agreement when he was engaged was that there should be a week's notice on either side.

"Plaintiff had grossly broken the rules of the island, and there was an evident amount of secrecy and suspicion about the gun, which was hidden beneath a bed wrapped up in an old article of clothing.

"Finding there had been such a breach of his rules, he submitted that defendant was justified in dismissing his servant without notice, especially as Williams had also threatened and sworn at him.

"Ezra Joseph Neale, the defendant, living at 24, Thomas Street, Bristol, said he was the lessee of St George's Island, Looe, under Sir William Trelawny.

"The rule book had not been altered in the slightest since he first handed it to plaintiff. He agreed to engage plaintiff at 16s a week, his wife being expected to cook and assist at his house without extra pay.

"Not a word was said about a month's notice. Plaintiff said, "I suppose it will be a week's notice or wages on either side?" and witness agreed with that.

"On Boxing Day he came down to the island for some shooting, and found several dead rabbits with shot inside. That caused him to suspect Williams.

"When he got to the island on January 22nd he sent Williams off to Looe for the letters, milk and errands as usual, and Mrs Williams he instructed to clean up his house.

"In the cottage he reserved a bedroom for his own visitors and another room as a store room. Therefore, the house was always open to him, and he had been inside several times since Williams had been caretaker.

"On the 22nd he requested PC Holloway to search the cottage for the ferret, nets, and cartridges he had missed; but, although he told him that the house was his, the constable said he could not do so without a search warrant.

"He (defendant) remained outside the house while Holloway went for Mrs Williams, and the witness Toms had stated that which was untrue in saying he went into the cottage, because the tide being high, the cliff completely hid the cottage from view of anyone on the beach.

"When Holloway came back he again urged him to make the search. He refused, but requested Mrs Williams about the missing articles, and the woman at last got somewhat excited and said "If you think the things are here, come in and see for yourselves."

"On that invitation Holloway and he went inside. He asked her if she had a gun there, and she answered "There's no gun here, and no cartridges."

"He rejoined, "I'm certain there is, because I have found shot rabbits on the island." After a little further pressure by himself and Holloway, the woman herself produced a few cartridges from under a table in the sitting room, saying "Joe (her husband) bought them."

"She then acknowledged, also, that there was a gun in the house, and going into Williams' bedroom, she pulled out the weapon from under the bed, where it had been wrapped up.

"It was in three pieces. Neither he nor Holloway entered that room or searched the house in any way. He told Mrs Williams that he should take away the gun, as it was against the rules to keep it on the island.

"When Williams came back, Holloway, Toms, Mrs Williams and himself were on the beach. Mrs Williams ran down to the water, and called to her husband, "Run the bloody boat on a rock and sink her," and then she told him that witness and the policeman had been searching the cottage.

"Williams jumped ashore, and began to pull off his coat, threatening to do for the --- (deleted expletive?) policeman.

"Mrs Williams said, "No; it isn't him; Neale's the worst." Then plaintiff was going for him, when Mrs Williams clung to him in a real or assumed hysterics.

"After that he (defendant) told Williams he should clear out at once. Plaintiff wanted to have a week's notice, but he refused, as his behaviour was so bad; he was cursing and swearing fearfully.

"He told his agent, Mr Scantlebury, to pay the man a week's wages. As to the revolvers in the cottage, he himself took one out of the sitting room, and Mrs Williams gave him the other with the cartridges.

"Cross examined: He expected Mrs Williams to assist in the housework when he was on the island. It was true that up to the time that Williams came he had two servants there, but they returned to Bristol with his family in September.

"Mrs Williams was assisted in the work of the house by one of his daughters. At the end of last year Williams wrote him that a gang of poachers from Looe had been round the island one night with nets, and he admitted sending the following telegram: "If necessary shoot them with ball cartridges, or into boat."

"That, however, was only a little bounce. The same day he wrote the following letter to Williams: "I am sorry to hear about the poachers. I telegraphed you to-day. You had better show the telegraph to the Looe people, and say you mean to shoot, and say that when your light is out you mean to be round the island in wait for them, etc, etc.

"If you tell a loud tale like that, it may prevent them coming again. Was it moonlight the night they were there? I expect they will land while you are in Looe. Don't, of course, tell that I told you to show (the) telegraph or to say so-and-so."

"Mr Venning: And was the letter all "bounce" too? - Defendant: I wanted to keep the poachers off the island.

"The Judge: What were the revolvers for? Were they all "bounce"? - (laughter).

"Defendant: No; I gave them to Williams to keep in his house, because he said he would be nervous on the island by himself.

"His Honour: How many chambers had they? - Defendant: One had six, and the other, I think, had seventeen or fifteen.

"In answer to further questions, defendant said he never touched any of plaintiff's papers or letters. From the appearance of the gun found in Williams's house it had been used for one or two seasons.

"Mr Venning: Did you ask PC Holloway to say that the gun had been fired; and he said he could not say that? - Defendant replied that he could not remember asking the constable to say so. Would not swear he did not. Had been lessee of the island for 15 years.

"Mr Venning: How many caretakers have you had during that time? - (defendant) - I don't know.

"Mr Venning: How many have you had in twelve months? Is it not a fact that you have been constantly changing? - (defendant) - I kept them as long as they behaved themselves. Two left because their wifes [sic] fell ill. I discharged one because his wife forged his name to three letters, and so got me to send two cheques. Another one used to stay in Looe drinking all day.

"Mr Venning: Now, shortly, do you know how many caretakers you have had on the island? - Defendant – No, I don't.

"The Judge: Considering that there are forty urgent rules in this rule-book to be obeyed, in addition to all ordinary rules, that would certainly be one probable cause of frequent changes. - (laughter)

"Mr Venning: yes; it appears to have been quite an autocracy.

"PC Holloway (Looe) said defendant fetched him to the island, alleging dishonesty against Williams; but witness refused to enter plaintiff's cottage, as he had no search warrant.

"Instead, he went to fetch Mrs Williams, leaving defendant outside the garden of the cottage, and he was in just the same place when he returned.

"Witness asked Mrs Williams if she knew anything about the ferret or the cartridges, and she replied, "We know nothing at all about it."

"After some more talk, she said, "Come inside if you think there's anything here."

"She was in a white heat of passion and said, "You shall come in; you shan't go back to Looe till you have seen for yourselves, or Neale will be sure to say we stole his things."

"Neale and he then went into the kitchen, but neither of them touched a thing. They continued to question the woman about the missing articles, and finally she produced the gun and seven cartridges, saying her husband had used the rest.

"Neale said he should keep the gun until he had a satisfactory explanation of how it came there. The woman then abused defendant, and threatened to slap his face. When they got on the beach, Mrs Williams, with an oath, called to her husband to sink the boat.

"Plaintiff jumped ashore, and made for witness. Mrs Williams said, "It's not him; it's Neale."

"Plaintiff threw off his oilskin coat, made for Neale, and there was a general melee for a few minutes, until Mrs Williams caught hold of her husband and nearly fainted.

"Neale told plaintiff he would have to leave his service that day, and Williams said he would take the notice and go.

"Afterwards he told witness more than once that he was only entitled to a week's notice, and that he blamed himself for not arranging for a month's notice when defendant engaged him.

"On February 3rd witness and PC Holloway accompanied plaintiff to the island at his own request while he fetched off his things, because, he said, he supposed he was only a trespasser there now.

"Cross-examined: By his Superintendent's orders he had since offered the cartridges again to plaintiff, because Neale could not identify them.

"Mr Venning: Who used the worst language on the beach that day - Neale or Williams?

"Witness: I shouldn't like to be able to swear like Williams did.

"Mr Venning: Did not Neale call Williams a thief and a rogue, and a poacher? (Witness) - Yes; but both of them were very excited.

"The Judge (to witness): Are you in the habit of going into houses without a search warrant? - Witness - No, sir; I have never been called upon before in such a case.

"His Honour: You had better not do it again. - Witness: But I never searched the house. I told the woman again and again that I could not search the house without a warrant. I only went inside when she told us we should not leave the island without seeing for ourselves.

"His Honour: I should advise you next time to do nothing of the kind, and not to enter a man's house while he is away, or you will get yourself into serious trouble.

"PC Holwill [sic] recounted a conversation with plaintiff in Looe street, and spoke to accompanying PC Holloway to the island on February 3rd, when plaintiff admitted being engaged only by the week, and said he knew guns were not allowed on the island. Thomas Scantlebury, agent for defendant at Looe for the past 18 months, said he had always been accustomed to pay the caretakers weekly.

"His Honour, in giving judgment, observed that the defendant, as the lessee of the island, seemed, in his own estimation, to be a sort of king and "the monarch of all he surveyed" - (laughter).

"His rules shewed [sic] that he was apprehensive of poachers, and his ground of complaint against the plaintiff was that he had been poaching, and had stolen a ferret, nets, and cartridges.

"Evidently, also, defendant was suspicious of the Looe people, as his third rule said: "Make no acquaintances with the Looe people, and have none of them on the island;" and, again: "Do not tell the Looe people that there are many rabbits here."

"It was clear, however, that plaintiff had read those rules, and therefore he was bound by them. Undoubtedly defendant had treated himself as Lord of the island.

"But he had lived a little too late. In the days of Robinson Crusoe and his man Friday he would evidently have been in his element. - (laughter)

"As to the first claim for unlawful entry, the rules themselves shewed [sic] that the cottage was the caretaker's own, and in speaking of the garden it said, "part of your garden." As the cottage must, therefore, be regarded as plaintiff's own, he was entitled to the protection of the great rule that "An Englishman's house is his castle."

"There was no more valuable or important rule than that in this world, and he should be sorry if any decision of his should ever have a tendency to whittle it away or invalidate it.

"Defendant, instead of behaving like a man and charging plaintiff with the theft of his goods, preferred to get the man off the island, and that of itself did not go to shew [sic] that he had a well-grounded complaint against him.

"The policeman in this matter seemed to have misunderstood his duty. He very properly told the woman that he had no warrant, but he followed her into the house and urged her to give up the things if she had them.

"He would not say positively, but he very much doubted whether a wife had the right to give permission to search her husband's house in the latter's absence; and in this case the woman was acting under coercion - the coercion of the majesty of the law as presented by the constable.

"Perhaps the most extraordinary feature of the case, however, was the fact of defendant taking away plaintiff's gun and carrying it off to Bristol. It was most unheard of conduct to confiscate a private person's property in such a way.

"The only thing that explained defendant's conduct was that, after a long occupation on the island, he had begun to imagine himself an absolute monarch, and accordingly arrogated to himself all the attributes of an autocrat.

"It was lucky for him that plaintiff was only claiming £5 damages. If he had claimed a good deal more he would probably have got it, both in that court or before a jury.

"As to the claim for dismissal without proper notice, he was satisfied that it was a weekly engagement, and that claim would be dismissed.

"On the former claim, however, judgment would be for plaintiff, with costs under scale C, on the ground that it was a case of great public interest.

"The decision was received with applause, which was immediately suppressed, the Judge saying he would have no demonstration of that kind, and if it was repeated he should clear the court.

"Subsequently Mr Childs applied of Mr Neale £3 12s 6d. for services rendered. Mr Venning explained that this claim was made in respect of domestic work done by plaintiff at defendant's house on the island, during nine weeks at the rate of 10s per week, less 17s 6d given plaintiff by Mrs Neale.

"Mr B. Childs again defended. - The Judge said he relied on the documentary evidence produced. No mention of the wife's services being required was made either in defendant's advertisement for a caretaker or in his letters engaging plaintiff's husband.

"He considered 5s a week a reasonable sum for her services, and gave judgment for £1 2s 6d with costs. He added, with reference to the former case, that he thought it due to the man Williams to say that there had been no sort of justification for the charge of theft brought against him by Neale."

All in all, it's an extraordinary account, of a most enlightening, and somewhat amusing case.

And it highlights interesting little facts about the island's wildlife – the apparent abundance of rabbits came as something of a surprise. There have never been wild rabbits on the island for as long as I've been visiting the place, and it's difficult to imagine how they might have ended up there naturally.

Perhaps they were settled there as shooting game. There seems a reasonable possibility that the woodland was planted for the same reason – to cultivate the island's shooting quarry.

Perhaps the Trelawnys had deliberately developed the island's habitat for use as a shooting and fishing retreat?

The court report certainly brings to life the rather feudal system that was at work on the island in the nineteenth century; with the owner (Trelawny), the lessee (Neale), and the caretaker (Williams).

The other interesting point from the report is the reference to Toms the island boatman. The Toms family (it seems fair to assume we're more than likely talking about the same Looe family) were still ferrying for the island even into the 1960s.

In her own notes, almost a century after the Williams vrs Neale case, Babs wrote: "From 1965 onwards, Reginald Toms, owner of the Orlando, takes oil and sacks of coal to the island, he beaches his boat at high water, unloads his cargo, and waits for the next high tide to enable him to get his boat off the sands."

Back at the end of the nineteenth century though, Neale's role as lessee had, it seems suffered something of a cursed incumbency – more than a decade before the Williams affair, his previous tenants on the island had been killed in tragic circumstances.

A faded note made by Babs in the 1970s, records (from an unknown source) that in 1883 a man called C H Leycester had rented the island for a term of four years from Mr Neale, but that tragically he, his wife, and their niece were all drowned while on a fishing trip.

Chapter 6
The Twentieth Century:
Living the Island Life

IT was a fine summer's day as I trudged up the spine of the island towards the chapel site.

The early morning sun was already hot on my back, and the first beads of sweat were glistening on my forehead, as I turned into the steepest section of the island's 150ft climb.

Stopping for breath, I lifted the basket of shearing tools off my shoulder, and placed it on the ground.

Looking out away from the climb the sea sparkled up at me, azure-blue and languid at the turning of the tide.

Seagulls cried overhead and the gentlest of breezes moved the tall grass with a whisper.

My eyes moved idly into the dense green tangle of the woodland beside me. I looked up at the pair of old metal reservoir tanks that stood on stilts above the woodland floor.

The drinking water, pumped from the shore-side spring, rests in the reservoirs, before being gravity-fed to the island's single tap in the "craft centre" – the kitchen area at the back of Jetty Cottage.

I was pondering how healthy the water could really be up in those moss-covered tanks, when I saw something I had never noticed before.

As my eyes adjusted to the woodland shadows I recognised a distinctive crater shape that stretched across the woodland floor. Covered with vegetation it wasn't at first obvious. But once you had seen it, the dip seemed quite pronounced – a circle, a couple of dozen feet across, and sinking to two or three feet in depth in the middle.

I had heard stories of the island having been bombed during the Second World War, but as I sat there looking at the crater the dark days of the 1940s seemed suddenly close.

It was clear that despite the sense of timelessness, the twentieth century had left its marks on the island, perhaps more than any century before.

Later I took the opportunity to ask Babs about the island's wartime exploits.

"It was bombed evidently," she said. "And people who know anything about the Second World War, would have heard of a man called Lord Haw-Haw. He was a British subject who acted as a traitor, and used to broadcast propaganda from Germany.

"He announced on one occasion that SS St George had been bombed, and actually it was a landmine that landed near the top of the island. But it broke all the greenhouses here, and greenhouses on Hannafore as well.

"There wasn't anybody living here during the war, although the military used the island a little – there was a gun emplacement at one time, we believe. You can see the concrete foundations for it by the jetty."

It must have seemed like a strangely remote outpost for some poor gunner during the war, despite the fact that it was so close to home.

I imagined a soldier, or a member of the Home Guard, sitting at the gun emplacement, and looking out at the empty sea – just like the old hermit three and a half centuries earlier, watching for the Spanish Armada from St Michael's Chapel on the other side of Whitsand Bay.

But 1940s watchmen would have been gazing out towards the Eddystone rock, never quite knowing whether a flotilla of Nazi ships were about to appear over the horizon.

The twentieth century had started more peacefully, with the island still in the hands of the Trelawny family.

According to the island's deeds, it was sold in 1921 to a Mr J.W. Topham and a Mrs E. Topham, before changing hands again within the same year to a Mr P. Corder.

But little seems to have actually happened on the island during the first half of the century, except for an incident that made the Cornish Times in 1929.

"It was one of the strangest things that must have happened here," Babs explained. "There was a whale washed up on Jetty Beach, and I have the cutting from the Cornish Times of the time.

"It was 56ft long, and 36ft in circumference. And it was dead of course, because once they've been beached they don't last.

"They didn't know what to do about it, so they sent to the local people in Looe, and they sent some men over to deal with it.

"We have a photograph of it, with six men standing on its back, with their hands joined together, and they don't go from end to end. There are two further men stood beside the whale, and there must have been an eighth man there to take the photograph. And these poor men were dressed in plus-fours, which makes for a very funny photograph.

"But in the end they decided to blow it up. They were paid five pounds to do this job, and they went back to the Jolly Sailor, to spend it on drink.

"They didn't know what type of whale it was, but they thought it would be interesting to find out. So they cut a lump of it, and sent it up to London to the museum to be identified. And this 100-weight lump of whale meat sat on Liskeard station. And everybody in Liskeard knew it was there – the smell was apparently very potent."

After the Second World War the island was turned once again to farming, as D-Day commander Major General S.B. Rawlings left the horrors of war behind him, and retired to the island's tranquillity (the Major General's surname is spelt as "Rawlins" on the island deeds, but Rawlings by Attie in We Bought An Island.)

"They ran it as a market garden," Babs said. "Then the price for early crops was very high, and he used to do potatoes and so on, that he could get good prices for on the mainland, being early crops.

"I'm not sure if he was the one who started the daffodils. We have very early crops of daffodils. In fact one particular variety we can pick before Christmas.

"When we first came we took on the marketing of daffodils, and we used to send them up to Miles at Covent Garden, and Attie and our friend Ruth, who was living with her at the time, used to pick them and bunch them, and send them over to me on the mainland.

"I had to be on the mainland, because I was teaching, and I did the boxing, and got up early in the morning to take the boxes up to catch the flower train at Liskeard. And I think there were 17 different varieties when we first came, but we've planted many more since then. At their best we had 37 different varieties of daffodils. Of course when I came, to me a daffodil was always yellow. But there's one particular one we've got which is pure white, and that used to command the best prices in London."

After surviving D-Day, Rawlings died suddenly on a train to Plymouth just a few years later. In 1957 the island was bought by Mr C. H. Whitehouse, a man with an unusual interest in monkeys.

The old, moss-covered stone monkeys that adorn the wall of the main island house are an echo of his time.

A very close inspection of the woodland, behind the Smuggler's Cottage, reveals the remains of a set of cages, in which, somewhat surreally, Mr Whitehouse is believed to have kept his own pet monkeys.

But the creatures met an ill-fated end.

"He had them up in the woods and he had a shed for them up there," Babs explained.

"And they went ashore one day, when it was cold, and left them with their usual oil stoves to keep them warm. But the monkeys knocked the oil stove over, and they were burnt to death, I'm afraid."

But it was the Atkins sisters themselves who left the greatest mark on island life for the twentieth century. The pair bought the island from Mr Whitehouse in 1964.

Babs was a schoolteacher and Attie had recently taken early retirement from her work in the personnel department at ICI's London headquarters.

But after a chance sighting of the island during a holiday to Cornwall, and the sudden discovery that it was on the market a few months later, the middle-aged sisters took the adventurous decision to leave their sedate Surrey life behind them.

In her book We Bought An Island, Attie recalled the moment she saw the island for the first time when walking on East Looe Downs.

"Below at last was the sea shimmering in the early morning sunlight, but what riveted my gaze in spell-bound astonishment was what I thought at first must be a mirage. There, beyond Hannafore, rising like a lost Atlantis out of the mist, was an island.

"Tender and green in the soft morning light it looked infinitely alluring as the mists melted in the rays of the rising sun. Enchanted, I took a photograph although I knew that no camera could capture the evanescent quality of the light or the magic of that moment."

A few months later the sisters discovered the island was on the market for £22,000, and although it was beyond their means, they arranged a visit.

Mr Whitehouse took to the sisters warmly, and offered to drop the price by £2,000, and even offered them a private mortgage of six and a half per cent, if they promised to conserve the island's natural wonders.

"Mr Whitehouse asked if we would be willing to make a covenant with the National Trust to protect the island from commercial development during any future ownership," Attie writes in the book.

"To this we readily and eagerly agreed for we too were anxious that this beautiful unspoilt gem should never be exploited for commercial gain."

Just a few years before they died the sisters transferred the covenant to the Cornwall Wildlife Trust, after much soul-searching, following the National Trust's decision to sell-off a number of its existing properties.

Back in 1964, the sisters' bravery continued as they chose to move onto the island during the winter months.

Attie recalled the storm that attacked their boat as they attempted to move their furniture from the mainland, with the help of local boatman Wren Toms:

"The rain lashed at us as we clambered on board. Darkness fell. Wren clad in oilskins and sou-wester had us all lined up, as with grim face he told us exactly what we were to do. "It is not just a question of saving the boat," he announced, "it is a matter of life and death!"

"He explained that we could not take off until there was sufficient water to float the Orlando. Tremendous seas were running in, crashing over us from the west and threatening to capsize us. The next moment they sucked back leaving the Orlando high and dry and, without the support of the sea, she was again in danger of keeling over. "Do what I tell you, instantly!" he ordered.

"At that moment a huge sea crashed down on us. "Everyone to the port!" yelled Wren. We hurled ourselves over to the other side of the boat. "To starboard!" roared Wren. And we all scrambled back again. We could not anticipate which way we had to throw ourselves for in that boiling sea the breakers came in all directions and Wren hung over the side judging to a nicety exactly where and when the next roller would break over us.

"We were not allowed to move except as ordered, for it would have upset the balance of the boat. We could see huge breakers creaming over the rocks even in the darkness, it was that wild. Rain poured down our necks in spite of sou-westers and oilskins, but we had so much implicit faith in Wren that in the short intervals we sat as though we were in a bus and Zena and I had a long discussion about piles, of all things, inspired by the fact that we were sitting in pools of an icy mixture of rain and sea water.

"And so we went on hurling ourselves to port or starboard as directed. There was no confusion as to which was which for we knew it was the opposite side to where we happened to be, we just pitched ourselves bodily across from one side of the boat to the other and hoped for the best."

Despite their urbane and sedate appearance, the sisters' bravery was tightly knitted into their DNA, as Babs told me during the 1999 interview.

"My father was particularly daring. When he was a lad, his grandmother thought that he was being brought up too soft, and she encouraged him to run away to sea. To help him she gave him a gold sovereign and a gold watch, and away he went.

"At that time of course, it was at the end of the last century, he went under sail, and he went round the world several times; rounded Cape Horn, and he was up in the riggings, and when he looked down all he could see was boiling sea.

"Another time he went to Valporezo, and he jumped ship there, and hoboed across America. I don't know if you know what hoboeing is, but it meant that he travelled on the tracks under the engine.

"He was with a pal as well, and the engine driver and guard got to know that they were there, and they were going to throw them off, until they said they had a pack of cards. So they let the lads go into the guards van, and they all played cards together.

"And that's how he got across America. Then he got himself a job as a cowboy, for a family who had two boys about his age, and wanted him to stay. But he wanted to get home to propose to my mother, he was so afraid she was going to be taken by somebody else. So he left, and came home, and they got married.

"We had a very happy childhood. I was the youngest. My sister was eight years older than I was, and I had two older brothers, and they were already out to work before I knew anything about them. It was a very happy family. My father adored my mother, and wouldn't look at anybody else at all. So I think that affected our family life a lot."

And the happy family life continued once the sisters had moved onto their island. It was only after they had started their new life that the idea of allowing the public to land came about.

Babs explained: "It was not our intention at all, we were just going to live on the island. But I got the job in Looe, which necessitated my staying on the mainland a lot of the time, and Attie was here alone.

"Come the summer she found people landing, and she didn't know how to cope with them. She didn't want to spend all her time on the beach, shouting 'get off, this is my island.' So she thought up a brilliant idea, that she'd put up a big notice to say there was a landing fee, and she thought this would frighten everybody away.

"Instead of which, of course, all the landladies in Looe sent all their visitors out to her, and she was stuck. Half a Crown I think she was charging, in those days. Then of course, everybody who set foot on the island wanted a cup of tea, and she didn't know what to do about that one. We'd had this room at the back of Jetty Cottage as a craft room, for actually making crafts. So she'd bring people in here.

"In fact the first people, she didn't know what to do with, and so she took them into our house, sat them in our lounge, made them a cup of tea in our kitchen, and took it into them. And she thought, well she can't do that everyday. So that's when she started to organise allowing people to come in here.

"She would make it in the house, and run down here with trays of tea, and she was exhausted at the end of the day. And then other people wanted lunch, so she was foolish enough to put on lunch for them. And she'd make scones for the tea as well, and all in all, it was very exhausting."

But outside the summer months, the island became an isolated place once again. After retiring from school life a few years later, the sisters spent many years with only each other for company during rough weather.

"But we never felt isolated really when we were together," Babs said. "I had a whole year here alone, after Attie died. And although I didn't care for Christmas, and a lot of people are alone for Christmas, I did feel a bit more cut off than most people I think. But it was bearable.

"And I never want to go to the mainland. I have to go occasionally to get to the dentist, or the optician, but if I could get away with one trip a year, I'd be happy."

But Babs admitted the winter months can be hostile.

"They can be very harsh," she said. "We've had hurricanes here. We had one very bad gale that coincided with the highest tide for three hundred years. It swept away parts of the main beach. Swept away the boathouse. Swept away two boats.

"And we had another hurricane – a south-easterly gale, which demolished some of the cliff. That fell down and destroyed the spring water pump. That was December, and we knew we wouldn't get anybody out at that time of the year, doing repairs. And it needed bulldozers and things, to take the cliff away, and get at the spring water.

"We had the storage tanks in the woods. So we knew that we had to keep going on the water that was in the tanks. We decided one cup of tea, and one cup of coffee a day. And it was a good job we did, because nobody came until March. Mind you, we had some homemade wine, so that helped."

But even that wasn't the most dramatic moment in the sisters' life on the island.

"No, I think the most dramatic moment was when we discovered that the cliff had fallen, we had no path, and we had to get up in the woods to get down to the beach, right round the back of the Smuggler's cottage," Babs said. "That went on for some time, before we could get the path rebuilt."

Babs believed living so closely with her sister on the island for so long brought them even closer together than normal siblings.

"We were a very united family," she said. "Attie and I got on very well. We had our moments, we quarrelled, but only about unimportant things. And they weren't really quarrels anyway. I think most families do. Adds salt and pepper to life doesn't it."

But in spite of all the dangers, Babs and Attie had an endearing love of island life.

In her 1986 sequel Tales From Our Cornish Island, Attie writes: "Babs and I had dreamed the impossible dream of owning an island, and by an incredible series of unforeseen events it had come about.

"For me it was fortuitous that I had retired early so was still active enough to take on what, to all our friends, seemed a daunting challenge. The island…although only one mile off the south Cornish coast, is pounded by wild seas for many parts of the year so at those times one might as well be 100 miles out in the Atlantic.

"…To those who enjoy the amenities of urban or suburban life, the prospect before us would have seemed incredibly primitive…As only island lovers the world over and through the ages would understand, we did not appreciate the paucity of our situation, for unbelievably it seemed to us that we had attained paradise. Heady with island fever, we saw everything bathed in a rosy glow of achievement…We were on our island... Nothing else mattered."

Babs was equally fond of their island home: "The worst part of island life is having to go ashore, shopping or to go to the doctor," Babs said. "I think that is the worst part. I can take anything the island throws at me, but not leaving it."

***

Even when Babs died in April 2004, she remained on the island – her grave was dug at the top of her beloved daffodil field, overlooking the jetty beach and the ever-changing face of the sea.

Now the island has entered a new chapter – and it has fallen to the conservationists of the Cornwall Wildlife Trust to maintain the delicate natural balance of this unspoilt little world.

If they manage as admirable a job as the island's dozens of incumbents over the past thousand years, they will be doing good work indeed.

"I hope that it won't change at all," Babs told me in 1999. "You can't say what nature's going to do about it, but as far as I'm concerned I think the island should always be owned by people who want to keep it as it is."

The Complete Interview with Babs:
Summer, 1999

IN the Summer of 1999 I spent an afternoon with Babs, sat in the Craft Centre on the island. We chatted, and after I had asked the questions I had on my notepad, she gave me more to ask her – stories she evidently wanted recording, like the tales of the craft work and pottery Attie had done on the island. This is the complete interview transcript in full.

Your parents were unusual in many ways?

"Yes I think they were. My Father in particular. Because when he was a lad, his grandmother thought that he was being brought up too soft, and she encouraged him to run away to sea, and to help him she gave him a gold sovereign and a gold watch, and away he went.

"At that time of course, it was at the end of the last century, he went under sail, and he went round the world several times; rounded Cape Horn, and he was up in the riggings, and when he looked down all he could see was boiling sea.

"And another time he went to Valporezo, and he jumped ship there, and hoboed across America. I don't know if you know what hoboeing is, but it meant that he was on the tracks under the engine. And he was with a pal as well, and the engine driver and guard got to know that they were there, and they were going to throw them off, and they said well they'd got a pack of cards. So they let the lads go into the guards van, and they all played cards together. And that's how he got across America.

"And then he got himself a job as a cowboy, for a family who had two boys about his age, and wanted him to stay. But he wanted to get home to propose to my mother, he was so afraid she was going to be taken by somebody else. So he left, and came home, and they got married. And they used to go to school together."

What are your memories of your childhood like? Was it a happy time?

"A very happy childhood, yes. I was the youngest. My sister was eight years older than I was, and I had two older brothers, and they were already out to work before I knew anything about them. I didn't know them as schoolboys at all. And they two got married, and I was bridesmaid at both of the weddings. It was a very happy family. My father adored my mother, and wouldn't look at anybody else at all. So I think that affected our family life a lot."

Then you went on to Cambridge after school?

"Yes, I went to training college at Cambridge, because I wanted to be a teacher. And that was great fun, because we could join in all the things that were going on in Cambridge."

Was it unusual at that time for a girl to study at Cambridge?

"I don't think it struck me as it was unusual. There were a lot of girls, especially at my college, but there were two women's colleges, as well."

What else did you do there other than studying? Did you act?

"Yes I did acting there, and, of course we had a lovely time on the Cam, with the boats there, but I didn't know I was going to live by water completely."

And when you left university?

"Then I got a teaching job in Surrey. It wasn't very near home, and it was the beginning of the war. I got a car so that I could travel there, because the journey by train was very difficult. And of course, then the war came, and it was most difficult to get petrol for the car. So we all tried to share journeys to help us out.

"And then of course, all the men got called up, and I found myself, although I'd been trained to teach all the subjects on the curriculum, we found ourselves doing all the men's work, like boys' PE, and taking their football games, cricket. Quite an interesting time. And that's when I did a lot of acting, and I joined a repertory company, and we'd go round doing troop shows. And that took us all round the country. I used to spend my weekend travelling up to Yorkshire, going to American airbases."

We know from Attie's books how you bought the island, but when did you realise that the plan was actually going to come together?
"I think straightaway, because it was during our summer holiday, that it was all agreed, and I went back to Surrey, to find a bank manager to lend us the other half of the money. I went back to teach, and handed in my resignation, which was at the Christmas - with no idea of how to get any income at all, because, I was giving up a big job. And I thought, well I'll get a teaching job somewhere in Cornwall, there's bound to be something of some sort, even if I travelled a lot, or had to stay away, because Cornwall is a very long county, and you can't always travel for long distances. And Looe's only at the very beginning of Cornwall.

"Strangely enough, three weeks after the term started, in the Time Educational Supplement, there was a job advertised, a similar job to my own, a deputy-headship, for a secondary modern in Looe. So I couldn't believe my luck. And I applied for it, and I didn't think I'd be called up even. But I was called for interview. And when I went to see the school in the morning of the day of the interview, there was somebody on the staff up for the job, and I thought, that's it, she's bound to be the chosen one.

"But luckily I got offered the job. So not only had we got an island, I'd got a job, and just a short distance off the island. Although it did mean of course, staying on the mainland, because I wouldn't have been able to travel daily - especially not in winter."

Had it always been an ambition of yours to live on an island?
"Well Attie I think was the keenest one, because she'd been inspired by the Isle of Wight - of all things, slight comparison! And we'd always visited islands - the one off Tenby, and Lundy. But it just seemed miraculous that there was an island here at all."

What do you think you would have done for the past 35 years, if you'd never seen the island?

"Just been stuck in a job I suppose, still commuting, and living in suburbia. Although it was a very nice part of suburbia, being on Epsom Downs."

And what did your friends and you family think about the move?
"Oh they were horrified, because for my sins, I used to organise a lot of parties. And they said: "Who's going to organise our parties?" and "you're going to miss all of your friends.""

What would you say are the worst parts of island life?
"Having to go ashore, shopping or to go to the doctor, I think that is the worst part. I can take anything the island throws at me, but not leaving it."

And how did you go about opening it up to the public?
"Now that was not our intention at all, we were just going to live on it. And then I got the job in Looe, which necessitated my staying on the mainland, and Attie was here alone, and come the summer she found people landing, and she didn't know how to cope with these people. She didn't want to spend all her time on the beach, shouting 'get off, this is my island.' So she thought up a brilliant idea, that she'd put up a big notice to say there was a landing fee, and she thought this would frighten everybody away.

"Instead of which, of course, all the landladies in Looe sent all their visitors out to her. And she was stuck. Half a Crown I think she was charging, in those days. Then of course, everybody who set foot on the island wanted a cup of tea, and she didn't know what to do about that one.

"We'd had this room as a craft room, for actually making crafts. So she'd bring people in here. In fact the first people, she didn't know what to do, and so she took them into our house, sat them in our lounge, and then made them a cup of tea in our kitchen, took it into them. And she thought, well she can't do that everyday. So that's when she started to organise allowing people to come in here.

"So she would make it in the house, and run down here with trays of tea, and she was exhausted at the end of the day. And then other people wanted lunch, so she was foolish enough to put on lunch for them. And she'd make scones for the tea as well, and all in all, it was very exhausting."

What features of the island lifestyle are you most fond of?
"Well, I think the gardening. That's the thing that attracts me, and in fact, I do that to the detriment of everything else. In other words I don't do any housework."

And do you ever feel isolated out here?
"No. I had a whole year here alone, after Attie died. And although I didn't care for Christmas, and a lot of people are alone for Christmas, but you feel a bit more cut off than most people I think. But it was bearable. It was bearable."

And do you ever feel you want to go to the mainland?
"No. Never. I have to occasionally to get to the dentist, or the optician, but if I could get away with one trip a year, I'd be happy.
"We were a very united family. Attie and I got on very well. We had our moments, we quarrelled, but only about unimportant things. And they weren't really quarrels anyway. I think most families do. Adds salt and pepper to life doesn't it."

How hostile are the winters here?
"They can be very harsh. We've had hurricanes here. We had one very bad gale that coincided with the highest tide for three hundred years. It swept away parts of the main beach. Swept away the boathouse. Swept away two boats.
"And we had another hurricane - a south-easterly gale, which demolished some of the cliff. That fell down and demolished the spring water pump. This would be December, and we knew we wouldn't get anybody out at that time of the year, doing repairs. And it needed bulldozers and things, to take the cliff away, and get at the spring water. And we had the storage tanks in the woods. So we knew that we had to keep going on the water that was in that storage tank. So we decided one cup of tea, and one cup of coffee a day. And it was a good job we did, because nobody came until March. Mind you, we had some homemade wine, so that helped."

How big a part of your life are your pets out here?
"I couldn't have stayed for that year without them. They're a great help. Nelson in particular is a very intelligent dog, and he jolly-well knows what I'm saying to him."

Do you ever regret having come out here?
"Oh no. It never crosses my mind at all. No regrets."

Can you pinpoint a most dramatic moment?
"Well I think really when we discovered that the cliff had fallen, we had no path, and we had to get up in the woods to get down to the beach, right round the back of the Smuggler's cottage, and that went on for some time. I think that was the most dramatic one."

Any plans to write your autobiography?
"I don't think so, no. I might add a few more tales to the island tales, but I don't think that my life would be interesting to anybody before I came here."

What's the earliest thing you know about the island?
"Well, we think that the Celts were here, we have no proof of it at all. But there was a chapel, at the top of the island, and we know that was there in 1200, because we have the list of the chaplains to the island, from 1200 onwards, which is on the wall of the Talland Church, which is just along the coast from here.

"But, from what we know, there was also a monastery built on Hannafore. But research has shown that our chapel on the island predated that, because two monks coming over to the island, to conduct a service were drowned, and it was under the abbey in Glastonbury, and they set up a chapel on the mainland so visiting monks didn't have to face the bad seas – they would have somewhere to go.

"The legend of Joseph of Arimathea coming here with the child Christ, there's no authenticity about that. But strangely enough, the seal for West Looe, is a boat with two figures in it, one large and one small. And whether that has anything to do with the legend, we don't know. But there must have been a reason for a chapel to have been built on the island itself."

What do we know about the chapel?

"Well, the only thing we know about it, is, there was a diagrammatic map of the island, and the coastline between Fowey and Looe, and according to this diagrammatic map, which came out in Tudor times, the island seemed to be dominated by the chapel. The chapel looked as large as the island. They've got a copy of that in the British Museum."

And what do we know about when the monks left?

"Well, I think it must have been the dissolution of the monasteries that finished it. And then it was farmed by various people. Two people who took over here were the son and daughter of a smuggler who lived on an island off Plymouth. And when he died they didn't like to move to the mainland themselves, so they moved house and came and lived on the island here. And carried on with their own form of smuggling, and she was known as Black Joan.

"And then they put the preventive men on the island. Whether our house was that house, that was built for them, we're not quite sure. But we think that the Smuggler's Cottage – in fact we realise that the Smuggler's Cottage is one of the oldest buildings, apart from the chapel, on the island, and is about contemporary with this building [the craft centre], which used to be a barn – about 1720, we've been told by somebody who judges the age of buildings, but we haven't any confirmation of that at all.

"And the island belonged to the Trelawny family at one time, and the present holder of the title, Sir John Trelawny, a good friend of the island, visits fairly frequently."

And there are a lot of legends around the smuggling?

"Yes. On the far side of the island, there is a big indentation, which leads to a cave, which is about 30 yards long. It's big enough for you, at high tide, to row a boat into. It does get silted up sometimes. It depends on what winter gales we have. But on the cliff above that there's a large stanchion. And it's our idea that the smugglers used to come into this little cove and use this stanchion to haul their goodies up out of sight of anybody in Looe."

And there's supposed to be a tunnel?

"Well there's supposed to be one from here across to Hannafore, the last house at Hannafore is called Monk's House, because in their garden wall they have little niche windows, which are survivors from the second monastery that was built over there.

"And there is a place there called Buoy's Quay, and it would be a suitable place for anybody to land, but the story is that the place is riddled with tunnels – but we haven't found any of them.

"One is supposed to go from there to Wallace Quay. And one fantastic one, was another one from here to East Looe. But the most fantastic one of all is one from here to Fowey, but it happens to be nine miles away. So, utterly ridiculous."

And there are a lot of stories about Black Joan?

"Black Joan, yes. She is one of those who lived in Smuggler's Cottage. And when the preventive men were put onto the island, we understand there were some smuggled goods in the cave on the far side.

"And they wanted to get rid of the preventive men. So she pretended that her boat had gone adrift, and she came up calling that she was losing her boat. And there was one preventive man here, and he looked out and saw that it was drifting away, so he got into his dinghy and rode out after it.

"As soon as he had set foot in that, they all set-to, to load the smuggled goods and hide them. And another thing in a very old book, a copy of the Cornish Magazine from 1890, somebody had interviewed one of the old smugglers from here. And he said that the smugglers used to bring their goods here. And the people who lived on the island, Black Joan and her brother Amram [sic], they didn't actually do smuggling themselves, but they hid the stuff for them, and they used to lock them in the cottage and hide the goods so that not even the smugglers knew where they were hidden."

And there's supposed to be some of that buried treasure left here?

"Yes. Before I came to live here permanently, my sister received a letter from a clergyman who lived in the Lake District, and he said he had been in the possession of a map that had been in his family for many years. His cousin had visited the island, and thought that we were the right people to have this map. And so he had sent it to us.

"It's a very old map, all the S's are F's. And every time you touch it, it breaks up. So we have it hidden very secretly, and it does show where the treasure is. We once did have a young fellow here, who spent his fortnight's holiday digging in what we thought was the place. But he didn't find anything."

And what do we know about the 19th century here?

"It belonged to the Trelawny family during that time. And I think they farmed it out, they gave people, allowed them to come here and stay and farm. And previous owners to us – this isn't 19th century, this is up to date – they ran it as a market garden and Major General Rawlings, who was a D-Day commander had it immediately after the war.

"Then the price for early crops was very high, and he used to do potatoes and so on, that he could get good prices for on the mainland, being early. And of course, I'm not sure if he was the one who started the daffodils. We have very early crops of daffodils. In fact one particular variety we can pick before Christmas. And when we first came we took on the marketing of daffodils, and we used to send them up to Miles at Covent Garden, and Attie and Ruth, who was living with her at the time, used to pick them and bunch them, and send them over to me.

"I had to be on the mainland, because I was teaching, and I did the boxing, and got up early in the morning to take the boxes up to catch the flower train at Liskeard. I think there were 17 different varieties when we first came, but we've planted many more since then, and at their best we had 37 different varieties of daffodils. Of course when I came, to me a daffodil was always yellow. But there's one particular one we've got which is pure white, and that used to command the best prices in London."

What do we know about the island during the Second World War?

"It was bombed evidently. And people who know anything about the Second World War, would have heard of a traitor called Haw-

Haw. And he was a British subject who acted as a traitor, and he used to broadcast from Germany. He announced one time that SS St George had been bombed, and actually it was a landmine that landed near the top of the island. But it broke all the greenhouses here, and greenhouses on Hannafore as well."

Who was here during the war?
"There wasn't anybody here during the war. There was a gun emplacement at one time, we believe. You can see the concrete foundations for it.

"We had two canon balls we found here, which must have come from some battle earlier on. I always tell the children they came from the Armada, but whether they did or not is anybody's guess. Because the first battle was off here. We have a book on the Armada which contains a contemporary map of the time, and it shows the crescent of the Spanish boats, just west of the island. And the English ones staggering out from Plymouth, having played their game of bowls. And our island is shown, but it was called St Michael's island then, on an older map it's St Nicholas', now it's St George's, and everybody calls it Looe Island.

"But we very religiously fly the flag, and we've been given a lovely new one by Gus and Sheila, who are living here now, and we fly that on St George's Day. I bet we're the only people in Cornwall who do. And we put it out for birthdays, and any other festive occasions.

"With the day visitors we allow, we only ever allow one boatman to come. Because we don't want the island spoilt, and too many people could not only wear-down the paths and so on, but wear-down us as well. So we only allow the one boatman. And I meet everybody that comes onto the island, so we never have strangers walking around. It makes an awful lot of difference. We don't provide rubbish bins, and nobody drops any rubbish. A lesson to be learnt by somebody I hope.

Wasn't there a story about one of the previous owners and his monkeys?
"Yes. In fact the previous owner to us, Mr Whitehouse, he had monkeys. And he had them up in the woods and he had a shed for

them up there. And they went ashore one day, when it was cold, and they left them with their usual oil stoves, and they knocked the oil stove over, and they got burnt I'm afraid."

Have you ever thought of keeping different varieties of animals yourself?
"We've thought about it. In fact our latest thought is to have red squirrels, but whether we've got the food that they would enjoy, I'm not quite sure. But it would be nice. You see we're very lucky the island's wooded, and that's an unusual thing for small islands. Usually they're too windswept to have trees. And in a book, Bond's History of Looe of 1823, he speaks about the island, and he says the island would be the better for trees. So there weren't any trees then. Whereas now of course, it's really quite fervent with the greenery. And it does mean we get woodland birds as well as seabirds."

And there are a lot of crafts going on, on the island?
"Well when we came here we were going to spend our time doing crafts, and as a matter of fact Attie did start off doing pottery. She knew nothing about pottery, and she went on a week's course in Devon, and the chappie who ran it, Paul Shelley, told her that she must get herself into a good arts school, because she had potential.

"So when we went back to Surrey, she went to the local school of art in Hexham, which had a very good reputation. And the normal course to become a potter is seven years, but she did about seven months I think. But they were very good people who ran it, they taught her much more than she should have learnt in the short time that she was there, and when she came down here onto the island, they came as well and we had nowhere for them to sleep, so they set up tents and slept in tents. And they left two of their advanced students to help her set up the pottery.

"And behind the generator room, is a huge room that was used when the generator was a DC system, and there were rows of accumulators on stone benches. So they ripped all that out, got rid of the accumulators, and built up concrete benches for her to do her pottery. And she bought a kiln. In fact she had one small kiln given to her as a retirement present when she left ICI, and then she bought a larger one. And she had a wheel built for her by a Dorset wheelwright, and set up various things there and started on her pottery.

"And she was really very successful, because she made her own glazes, which was really very unusual. Most people buy their glazes. But she wanted to get her own glazes. And she used to do little tiny bits of pottery with all the different glazes at different temperatures, and saw the results and decided which ones she liked, and she went on from there. She was very anxious that she should try to do her best, and as I say, she did have the help of these two young potters to begin with, and they were in their seventh year of learning pottery. Mr and Mrs O'Neil also, who ran the pottery school, were very good as well. And I think she produced some good pottery considering her lack of long experience."

How do you get your electricity and water?

"We're very lucky, we've got a spring. Most little islands of this size don't. In fact we have a friend who lives on an island in Scotland, and it's got many inhabitants, and they have to get their water from a nearby island. And in Scotland they don't work on a Sunday, so they get no water on a Sunday. But we have a spring of our own.

"When we first came the pump that we had to use to pump up the water, was one that you had to pull a string. You'd walk up some steps off the beach, because the spring was in the cliff on Jetty Beach. And if the string broke, you fell backwards down the steps. But now we have an electric pump, which is much more modern and up to date. And touch wood, it hasn't let us down lately.

"It is pumped up to tanks in the wood, they're storage tanks, and it's gravity-fed to each of the buildings. And now we have day visitors of course, there was a great drain on our spring water, for things like lavatories, and we have helpers who come and stay for the summer with the visitors, and that was a drain on our spring water. So we made up our minds that the spring water should be kept for the most essential things, like drinking and cooking, and wine making. And then we use rainwater.

"There were two main barrels when we got here. We've got 37 now. And we use the rainwater for washing ourselves, and washing up, and the laundry. And then we pump up seawater for the lavatory, and I haven't found anyone else in the country who uses seawater for lavatories. If there are, I'll be glad to meet them."

What about electricity?

"That's a generator. This is our second generator, there was one here when we came – a small five kilowatt one. But there's a limit to what you can get from it, and we were anxious that Attie should be able to do her pottery by electricity. So we made enquiries, and when we could afford it, we had a bigger, seven kilowatt one put in.

"And we have the five kilowatt one now as a stand-by, and that's pretty ancient, because we've been here 34 years, and it had been here some time before that. And with the tender guidance of Guss, it hasn't caused us much trouble lately."

There are a number of beaches here. You must have had some strange things washed up over the years?

"Not in our time, but one of the strangest things that must have happened here was a whale washed up on Jetty Beach, and I have the cutting from the Cornish Times of the time, 1929 it was.

"And it was 56ft long, and 36ft in circumference. And it was dead of course, because once they've been beached they don't last. They didn't know what to do about it, so they sent to the local people and they sent some men over to deal with it. And we have a photograph of it, with seven men standing on its back [actually six men on the whale, and a further two standing beside it], with their hands joined together, and they don't go from end to end. So there must have been an eighth man there to take the photograph. And these poor men were dressed in plus-fours, which makes for a very funny photograph.

"But in the end they decided to blow it up. They were paid five pounds to do this job, and they went back to the Jolly Sailor, to spend it on drink.

"And they didn't know what type of whale it was, but they thought it would be interesting to find out. So they cut a lump of it, and sent it up to London to the museum to be identified. And this 100-weight lump of whale meat sat on Liskeard station. And everybody in Liskeard knew it was there – the smell was apparently very potent.

"Another strange thing that came up on the beach was when we were here, or at least when Attie was here by herself. It was a china owl. It came floating in over the water, and she rescued it. And apart from a tiny little chip on one of its wings, it was perfectly undamaged. It had a plastic bag pushed up its innards, and I think that helped it to float. It was a piece of Beswick pottery, and it really is quite a pleasure to look at."

And somewhat more tragically though, there was a body washed ashore?

"Yes, that was unfortunate, because it was somebody that we knew. Soon after we came here, I had my niece and nephew come to live on the island to help run it. And they had three small children, who needed to go to school. So I had them over with me on the mainland, and I looked after them.

"And of course I had a lot of commitments as a teacher, and I had evening commitments that I had to go to. So I had to have somebody to look after the children for me when I was out. And this person used to come regularly. Whenever I needed her she came and baby-sat for me.

"But she got a little bit elderly and a little bit distressed, and evidently she went wandering through the streets of Looe in her nighty one night, and fell in the river. And her body was washed up on the island. It was somebody who worked for us at the time, Jack, he found her one Sunday."

How would you like to see the island evolve in the years to come?

"I hope that it won't change at all. You can't say what nature's going to do about it, but as far as I'm concerned I think the island should always be owned by people who want to keep it as it is. And that's why I'm so very anxious that it will not get into the hands of private people who want to exploit it in any way, and that it belongs to a trust that has the same ideas as Attie and I had when we started."

Island Pictures

David Clensy with Babs Atkins in 1999

The island seen from near the Ranneys
(picture: D Clensy 1997)

Caves at the back of the island were once used by smugglers
(picture: D Clensy 1997)

The late Dave Gardener, ferryman to the island
(picture: D Clensy 1996)

Gulls nest on Little Island
(picture: D Clensy 1998)

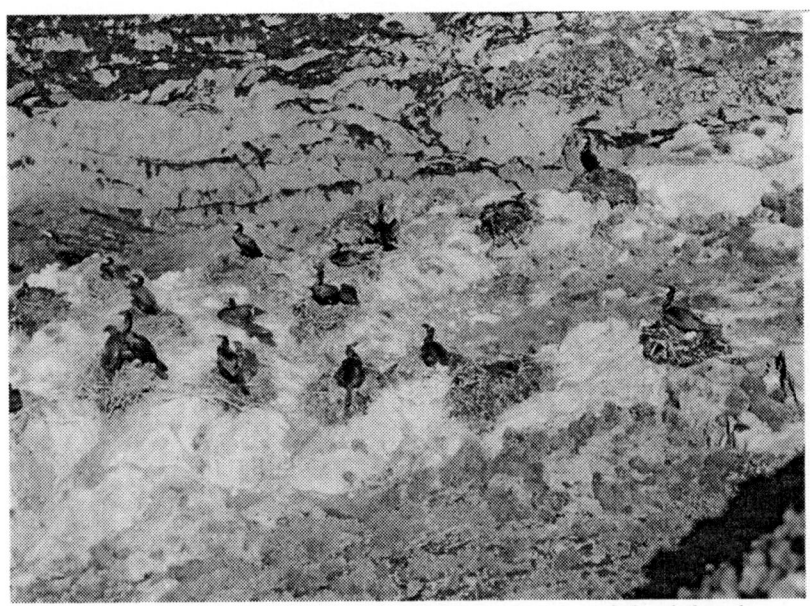

Cormorants nesting on the seaward side of the island
(picture: D Clensy 1998)

Island House
(picture: D Clensy 2004)

Smuggler's Cottage
(picture: D Clensy 1993)

Monastic remains on the island's chapel site
(picture: D Clensy 1993)

Tourists take a look at the island
(picture: D Clensy 1997)

Concise Bibliography

A Book of The West Cornwall, S. Baring-Gould (1899)
Looe and South Cornwall, Ward Lock (1953)
Vanishing Cornwall, Daphne du Maurier (1967)
Joseph of Arimathea, Isabel Hill Elder (1999)
Did Our Lord Visit Britain as they say in Cornwall? Rev C.C. Dobson (1936)
Total Community, The Monks of Caldey Island, Roscoe Howells (1975)
The Confident Hope of a Miracle, Neil Hanson (2004)
We Bought An Island, Evelyn E. Atkins (1976)
Tales From Our Cornish Island, Evelyn E. Atkins (1986)
The Story of Britain, Roy Strong (1997)
A Story of Looe Island, J Roger Hunt (1966)
The Isles, Norman Davies (1999)
Topographical and Historic Sketches of the Boroughs of East and West Looe, Thomas Bond (1823)
Rambles Beyond The Railway, Wilkie Collins (1851)
A Tour to the West of England, Rev S. Shaw (1788)
Early Tours in Devonshire and Cornwall, R. Pearse-Chop
Dissolution of the Monasteries, G.W.O Woodward, (1993)
A Famous Smuggling Craft, Commander H.N. Shore (1890)
Smuggling Days and Smuggling Ways, Commander H.N.Shore (1929)
History of Cornwall, Lakes Par (1870)
The Parochial History of Cornwall (1938)
Tudor Cornwall, A.L. Rowse (1941)
Cornish Magazine
New Penny Magazine
Cornish Times
Shapcott Lectures (1928)
The Order of St Benedict website - www.osb.org
The Online Catholic Encyclopaedia – www.newadvent.org
Britannia Online Encyclopaedia – www.britannia.com/history
Barbara Birchwood-Harper, curator of Looe Museum – www.looeoldcornwallsoc.com

Also by the author:

The Mole of Edge Hill:
The World of Williamson's Tunnels

Williamson's Tunnels remain one of Liverpool's most intriguing mysteries, some two centuries after they were constructed by the city's greatest eccentric, Joseph Williamson.

In the early years of the nineteenth century this rich merchant paid a secret army of men to dig a labyrinth that stretches for miles beneath the city.

In The Mole of Edge Hill writer David Clensy presents a dual approach to understanding more about this singular character.

The first half of the book is a short novel in which the author brings the eerie subterranean world to life, imagining what Williamson's life may have been like.

In the second half of the book, the writer presents the most in-depth history yet written of the real Mole Of Edge Hill.

Available from www.amazon.co.uk and all good book shops

or direct from the publishers at www.lulu.com

Reviews of Island Life: A History of Looe Island:

Oscar Morse, Cornish Guardian:
... a fascinating book about the colourful history of this Cornish landmark ...

John Weller, Hull Daily Mail:
The author's love of the island shines through his well-researched, atmospheric narrative ... reminiscent in style of travel writer Michael Palin ...

www.looeisland.com

www.davidclensy.com